HEDGEHOGHAVEN

Or

'A Yank & his Dog in England'

By

HELLS LEFSE

The World's Greatest Unknown Author

Table of Contents

DEDICATION

To my canine partners Tesse and Julio, whose love and devotion are shown to me every hour of every day.

It is with a sad and broken heart that I have to announce that Tesse has passed away. This book was told by her and in its final stages of being finished. Many tears were shed by me as I wrote the last few paragraphs.

Always in my heart and my memories with love

Sven 2006-2022

Lena 2007-2022

Tesse 2008-2023

In Memoriam

To one of the biggest fans

My Brother

Dale G Olson

1947-2021

DISCLAIMER

To all or any of you who happen to read this book please take note that Hells Lefse does the proof reading. Any errors are either intentional or unintentional depending on the mood he is in. If you think any fictional character in this book resembles you then that would mean that you are also fictional. If you find any spelling, grammatical or fictional mishaps, please address your comments, complaints or praise directly to Hells.

OTHER BOOKS BY HELLS LEFSE

Dogpire

Dogoyles

SvenSagas

Zomdoggies

Drogons

Booger Fairy

Buffole

Drogons 2

Sven Kabone

Drogons 3

Buffole Robyn Deadwood

Drogons 4

Buffole the Legend of Coyote Carol

Buffole Legend of the Golden Buffalo

Thanks a Slot

Drogons 5 The Final Saga

Deadwood Desperado's

CHAPTER 0

Hedgehoghaven. A village tucked away in the secluded county of Longhall, England. Bordered on three sides by the modern world and on the other side by the sea. A village is known by few, and it prefers to remain so. The occupants are a bit quirky, and they believe in living in their own little secluded world that is little affected by the happenings of the present day. The best way to get there is by a seldom-used railroad branch line that is owned by the county of Longhall. It connects with the mainline for the transfer of goods and occasional passengers. However, there is a narrow one-land road that leads out of the village to a main thoroughfare that will connect the driver and his vehicle to the modern world. Of course, the majority of the residents would wonder why anyone would ever want to do that.

Now let me introduce myself. I am going to be your guide and storyteller for this saga of Hedgehoghaven and its surrounding county. My name is Tesse, and I am a cute as a button white and tan Shih Tzu dog. Yes, you read that correctly. I am of the canine persuasion, and through a fluke of nature and maybe a gift from God, I am able to read and write, and best of all, I can communicate with my human partner Ole. I can relay my thoughts to him, but unfortunately, he has to talk out loud to communicate his thoughts to me. Of course, this means I can understand all other humans, and contrary to the old adage that some humans are dumber than animals, there are many animals that are smarter than humans.

So, from a dog's point of view, let's move on to chapter one and some important information to help you keep things straight. Just for clarification, I am writing this as an American canine, so please forgive any errors that I may make as to the speech and or attitudes of our English cousins.

CHARACTERS IN ALPHABETICAL ORDER:

Archie, owner of the Pastry Shop and Bakery. Married to Queen Bee, constable

Carl, Deacon of St. Catherine's Church

Caraline, Valerie & Kelley's daughter, owner of Caraline fishing boat

Carol, owner Carol's Stables and Penny & Pound Bank, Steve's sister

Casey, owner Chaps Pub married to Tracey, 3 daughters Tessa, Erica, Olivia

Current, Hedgehog who live near the Poachers Rest cottage

Dale, Hedgehoghaven's Fire Chief

Doug, owner Dingmann's Clothier for Men & Women store and the Mortuary

Eleanor, co-owner Bulldog Café with twin sister Rosemary, daughter of Henry & Nikki

Eastman, owner of Eastman mine

Erica, owner Pickwick Books Shoppe Casey & Tracey's daughter

Guido, street organ grinder with monkey name Nickoleno

Henry owner Henry's Hardware and General store. Married to Nikki, son Oscar, twin daughters Rosemary & Eleanor

Kaylynn, Kelley & Val's daughter

Kelley, owner Kelley's Arcade, married to Val, daughters, Kaylynn, Caraline, Victoria

Kevin, owner Kilroy's Slot Shop, nick name Kilroy

Kilroy, nick name of Kevin

Lates, Hedgehoghaven's Post Man

Merriweather Fische, solicitor of legal firm Fische & Chipps

Nikki, owner Hotel Hedgehog aka Kings Head Hotel, married to Henry, three children, Oscar, Rosemary & Eleanor

Nickoleno, monkey that works with Guido the street organ grinder

Ole, American who inherits Longhall county and town of Hedgehoghaven and Longhall Manor. Owns and operates Ole's Odditorium. Tesse's human companion. Now Lord of Longhall County

Olive, owner of Olive's Café, married to Roger

Olivia, Casey & Tracey's daughter runs a fishing boat supplying fish to the village

Oscar, Owns Hobby shop and help's his dad Henry at Hardware store

Pete, Police Sargent

Pierce, owner of the puffer ship Carolsea, also known as Captain Pierce. Brother to Roger & Winton

Queen Bee, junior police constable, married to Archie

Ray, owner of Lovitt's Butcher shop

Roger, foreman of Hedgehoghaven railway, brother to Pierce & Winton

Rosemary, co-owner Bulldog Cafe with twin sister Eleanor, Henry & Nikki's daughter

Steve, owner Oast Hops & Brewery, also known as Whiskey Steve, Carol's brother

Tessa, owner Tessa's Tea Shop, Casey & Tracey's daughter

Tony, owner Tony's Repair Shop

Tracey owner Tracey's Fruits and Vegetables store. Married to Casey, Daughters Tessa, Erica & Olivia

Val, owner Val's Natural Healing & Massage, married to Kelley, daughters Kaylynn, Caraline, Victoria

Victoria, owner Victoria fishing boat, daughter of Kelley & Val

Winton, owner of In Cod we Trust restaurant & smoked fish store, Pierce & Roger's brother

UNUSUAL ITEMS

Hedgehog Beer, local brew from Whiskey Steve's Oast Brewery

SvenBrew & SvenSoda. Special beer invented by Sven the Shih-Tzu dog contains raspberries, cherries, and a puppy dog's kiss, tail wagging good. Beer is served with three green olives.

Lena's SummerWine. Invented by Lena the Shih-Tzu dog. Made of raspberries and lemon.

CHAPTER 1

My human Ole and I were lounging around on the dock with not much going on around us. It was June 30th; the temperature was 88 degrees with no breeze. Ole sat on the dock's bench, occasionally sipping a drink from the warm glass bottle of Squirt that sat in the deck benches drink holder. As for me, being a canine, I'm a bit smarter than some humans, and I prefer to lie under the bench in the shade. A few dragon fly's flittered about, but for the most part, it was even too hot for the insects to be stirring around. Ole likes the sun and doesn't seem to mind the heat. He says it makes his bad back and busted-up leg feel better.

After about thirty minutes of cooking himself, Ole suggested we go for a swim. He had on shorts and a Little Rascals t-shirt that said 'He Man Woman-haters club.' It had special meaning for him due to his past experiences with the opposite sex. One thing to take note of is in our household; there are still only two sexes, male or female. I being of the female persuasion, should be offended by that t-shirt. However, I'm not a human female, I'm a canine female, and Ole has never had issues with the female canine sex. Of course, that's because we are faithful and loyal, and we won't up and leave you just because the grass or, in our case, the dog food looks better on the other side of the fence.

Ok, back to going swimming. Ole stripped off his t-shirt and waded into the lukewarm Mississippi River. I was right behind him, and he squatted down so I wouldn't have to be in deep water. The two of us frolicked and played for a bit, and then Ole moved up by the shore so I could sit next to him in the water. A few boats went by along with an occasional personal watercraft which Ole always made sure he told me which brand it was as his job as a salesman in the power sports industry made that one of his many subjects of interest. He was always quick to point out any Honda Aquatrax that we saw as they were, in his mind, the best watercraft ever built.

Ole: "Wait here a minute Tesse. I'm going to get a lawn chair for myself, and then I can sit here in the water with you and read a book out loud so you can hear. That way, I don't have to worry when a boat goes by about getting the book wet."

Once Ole was settled in, he opened the book and started to read from where we had left off. It was a book called 'Thanks a Slot' by the world's greatest unknown author Hells Lefse. I would assume, by being the greatest unknown author, that absolutely no one bought his books, except maybe Ole and me.

We were only a few pages into the book when we heard a car door slam. I asked Ole if he heard it.

Ole: "I did."

"Don't you think maybe we should see who it is?"

Ole: "You can go see if want to. I don't really care. You know, no one ever comes to visit. It's probably the mailman or some other delivery person."

"Their vehicles don't have doors like cars, so they don't slam them. I think we should go check."

Ole: "You go check. I'll stop reading until you get back."

I got on to the shore and shook the water off my coat; running up to the driveway, I saw a taxi cab parked on the driveway of the L-shaped part of the house so it was not visible from the river. A man was standing by the door pushing the doorbell and looked rather impatient that no one was answering the door. I looked him over and wasn't quite sure what to think. He was dressed in what looked to be a very conservative yet very expensive tailored suit. He had a briefcase in his hand and a bowler hat on his head. Small round glasses balanced on his pointy nose. Overall he had a look of somewhat comical dignity. Sure as heck, he wasn't a Jehovah's Witness.

I gave a bark at him, and he turned and saw me.

Man: "Well, well, little dog. Who are you? Do you live here? If so, where is your master?"

He talked as if he figured I might understand him, which I did, but I wasn't going to talk back to him; that right was reserved for Ole and me. However, I did run to the corner of the house and looked back to see if he would follow. He hesitated for a minute, so I barked again and ran a few more steps to get him to follow me. Sometimes humans are sort of slow to follow instructions from a dog. The cab driver was a bit smarter, and he told him that I wanted him to follow me.

Man: "Really, you think that animal is smart enough to want me to follow it?"

Cab Driver: "Of course, it's smart enough. Haven't you ever owned a dog? There a lot smarter than some humans."

I could see the cab driver smirking that the man was so ignorant of the ways of dogs.

Man: "Well, I suppose it won't do any harm to follow the beast for a little way. Maybe it will lead me to its master."

Cab Driver. "Maybe."

Man: "You wait here until I return."

Cab Driver: "No problem. I'll keep the meter running."

I went slowly enough for the man to keep me in sight as he followed me down to the river. Ole was still sitting in his lawn chair with his eyes closed and just soaking up the sun without a care in the world. I jumped the small gap of the open area from the grass to the dock and then sat down facing Ole. The man soon joined me. He looked at Ole; then he looked down at me as if he was waiting for me to do something about the man who looked to be asleep sitting in a lawn chair in the water. I figured I might as well take over for the moment, so I gave a loud bark.

Ole: "Tesse, you finally came back. Was it some delivery guy?"

Ole still had his head back, and eyes closed as he spoke, so I barked again as the man next to me said, "Ahem. Sir, may I speak to you?"

Ole finally opened his eyes and turned his head towards the dock. I could see he was as surprised at the man's attire and looks as I had been.

Ole: "Of course, if you don't think it will wrinkle your suit feel free to have a seat on the edge of the dock."

Man: "I do believe I would prefer to stand, sir. Let me introduce myself. My name is Merriweather Fische of the firm of Fische and Chipps solicitors of law from London, England."

Ole let out a laugh, as did I; of course my laugh was silent but openly visible by the quick wagging of my tail.

Ole: "Fish and chips, really, you must be kidding me. Who put you up to this? Has to be someone I know well as fish and chips is my favorite meal."

Mr. Fische: "Sir, I assure you this is no prank. Our firm really is called Fische and Chipps. Spelled F-i-s-c-h-e and C-h-i-p-p-s. I have here in my briefcase some very important documents that I would like to discuss with you. I have travelled very far, and I have a taxi whose meter is running, waiting for me in your driveway. So, if you would not mind giving me a few moments of your time and somewhere with a table that we can use so I can go over the documents with you, I would be very grateful for your cooperation."

Ole: "Sure thing there, Merriweather. Let me put my chair in the boathouse, and we'll go up to the dining room of the house, and you can show me what you got."

I communicated my thoughts over to Ole. "I think this guy might be for real. Whatever it is he has to show us might be important. Try to be a bit more sophisticated; you're embarrassing me. Also, don't call him Merriweather; address him as Mr. Fische."

Ole looked at me and mouthed the words, "What? How am I not being sophisticated?"

"You're making him wait while you put your chair away. He has a cab waiting, and what's with the show me what you got, that's not proper English, and you know it. You talk like a kid from the Our Gang shows."

Ole glared at me as if he didn't like me scolding him like a child. After all, he was acting like one. We had no idea what this was all about, and it might just be worthwhile if this fellow was who he said he was.

We entered the door of the walk-out basement, and I was pleased to see Ole hold the door open for Mr. Fische. Ole politely pointed the way up the stairs and followed along behind, as was the proper thing to do for a guest. We made our way to the dining room table, and Ole actually pulled out a chair for Mr. Fische and asked if he would like something to drink.

Mr. Fische: "A spot of tea would be nice if it's not too much trouble."

Ole: "Well, Mr. Fische, I do have some tea I got when I was in China, but to be perfectly frank, I do not have the slightest idea as to how to make it. I don't even have a coffee pot, much less a teapot."

I think this made Mr. Fische relax a bit, and he offered to make the tea himself.

Mr. Fische: "May I use your microwave to heat some water?"

Ole: "Feel free to use anything you want. I do have sugar or lemon if you want some. I seem to remember from some British movies I have seen that some of you chaps, as they say, use it."

Mr. Fische: "No, thank you. Just the tea will be fine."

Ole: "I do have an assortment of sodas if you would like one with your tea. I have Squirt, 7-up, Nehi Grape, Svensoda, Mountain Dew, and Pepsi. "

Mr. Fische: "No, thank you, the tea will be fine."

Ole: "It's pretty hot outside. Would you mind if I took a soda to the cab driver while he is waiting?"

Mr. Fische: "I am sure the gesture would be appreciated. Please hurry back as the cab driver has told me he is keeping the meter running, and it would not do to waste any more money than necessary."

Ole: "Will do; I'll be back in a jiffy."

Mr. Fische had finished making his tea and was just sitting down when Ole returned. Ole poured me a small bowl of milk and set it on the table for me as he popped off the cap of his bottle of Squirt with his handy dandy 'cap gun,' as he called it. It was actually a bottle opener shaped like a gun with a spring-loaded mechanism that allowed you to shoot the bottle cap across the room. Which, of course, Ole did with aplomb as he shot the cap into a candy bowl on the kitchen counter.

I noticed Mr. Fische raise an eyebrow of surprise that I was served my drink and allowed to use the table just like a human, but he being a man of sophistication and manners, declined to comment on what to him must have been a severe breach of etiquette.

Ole: "Pretty good shooting, huh, Mr. Fische?"

Mr. Fische dryly answered. "Very good indeed, Mr. Ole."

Ole: "I've got extras of these cap guns if you want one or even a few extras for your partner or as gifts. Oh, and my name isn't Mr. Ole; it's just Ole."

Mr. Fische: "Your offer of the cap guns is most generous, but I believe it would not be an appropriate item to have in our solicitor's office. It would also not be proper for me to refer to you as Ole. Now, we really must get down to the business at hand."

Ole: "That sounds like a good idea. I must admit you do have my curiosity aroused."

Mr. Fische: "As well it should be. It took a considerable amount of time to track you down. I must say I am relieved that we finally found you, for this assignment has been a long and tedious one.

Mister Ole, it seems you are the closest living relative to your late great-grandfather Aaron Long of the county of Longhall, England. Your great-grandfather passed away almost a year ago, and in his will, he left everything to you. It seems he had come to the colonies when you were a mere lad to visit his daughter, your grandmother. As fate would have it, he seems to have fond memories of you. Unfortunately, he did not have an address; he knew only that when he was here that you were living in Minnesota, his memory was shadowy on any other facts other than to say it was somewhere in the middle of the state.

Although we are fairly certain you are the person we are looking for, I would like to ask you a few questions just to verify that our research is correct."

I was trying my best to hold back my enthusiasm, but the wagging of my tail hitting the spindle of the wood-backed dining room chair gave me a way to Ole as he heard the quickening thump-thump-thump of my tail hitting the wooden spindle.

Mr. Fische: "First off. What was your mother's maiden name?"

Ole: "Long."

Mr. Fische: "Your grandmother's maiden name; of course, all these questions are geared towards your mother's side of the family just to erase any confusion."

Ole: "Hall."

Mr. Fische: "Can you tell me the professions of your grandfather and grandmother and how many children they have, and are any still living?"

Ole: "My grandfather was a barber, grandmother was a beautician. Children, let me think for a moment. Six, they had six children, five girls, and one boy. They are all deceased."

Mr. Fische: "Do you have any recollection of meeting your great-grandfather?"

Ole: "Wow, I suppose a no would be a bad answer. But my dad told me if I didn't lie, I won't ever have to remember what I said. I really don't have any recollection of him at all."

Mr. Fische: "Well, I do believe that you have answered all my questions to our firm's satisfaction."

Bow-wow. My tail started beating that old chair spindle like I was a lumberjack cutting down a tree. We were going to be rich. Well, hopefully. I wonder what old great-grandpa left us. A fortune in cash, or maybe a castle in England. Or both. If it's a castle, I hope it's not haunted. I've seen too many scary old movies of damp, dreary English castles that were haunted by ghosts from England's bloody past. Maybe if it is a castle, it has a dungeon filled with unspeakable devices of torture. Ole loved old horror movies, he might think that would be great, but me, I'm not so sure. Oops, Mr. Fische is looking over some more papers. Best I listen in just in case Ole might miss something.

Ole: "To your firm's satisfaction. Exactly what does that mean? I'm not the guy you're looking for, or I am the guy you're looking for?"

Mr. Fiche: "Mister Ole, I do believe you may be the person we have been searching for. Of course, nothing is certain until I verify it with my partner Mr. Chipps at our home office."

Mr. Fische looked at his watch and shook his head as he made a tsk, tsk sound. "Mister Ole, I am afraid our time is up. I need to return to the room I have at the Holiday Inn for an important conference call with my partner in London. I do hope you will excuse me. We can resume our discussion tomorrow either here or over lunch in town. If you did not mind, I would like to eat somewhere with a local flavor to experience a bit of your Yanks down-home color, the wild west, like in the movies, would certainly tickle my fancy. A local place that would have some of your American dishes and yet allow us the privacy to go over your great-grandfather's last will and testament."

Ole: "Local color, huh? American food? I know just the place, and it's not too far from the Holiday Inn. I can even pick you up and drive you to the airport if you like."

Mr. Fische. "That would be splendid. I am flying out at three o'clock in the afternoon your time from the local airport. I believe they refer to it as the St. Cloud Airport. From there, I go to the Minneapolis-St. Paul airport, then to Chicago, and then back to England. A good hearty meal before I leave may help to alleviate the long flight home. As you know, airport terminals and airplane food both leave a rather nasty taste on one's palate."

Ole and I had flown a few times, and we both sort of liked airport terminal food, stuff like hamburgers, fries, sweet rolls, and snacks. However, Mr. Fische was right about airplane food. It wasn't fit for even human consumption, more or less than for a dog.

Ole: "What time would you like me to pick you up, Mr. Fische?"

Mr. Fische: "It will probably take the good part of an hour to go over the documents. I would like to be at the airport at least two hours before my plane is to take off. You know how tiresome it can be traveling in this day and age with the threat of terrorists, viruses, and so many other unforeseen obstacles. I suggest you pick me up at 11:00 am sharp."

Well, we weren't much on international travel, although we had been to China once. However, that was four years ago before the world had turned itself upside down.

Ole: "We'll be there. You be ready."

Mr. Fische: "I will be waiting for you in front of the Holiday Inn at 11:00 am. When you said 'we' would be there. You were not suggesting that you were bringing your dog with you?"

Ole: "Where I go, Tesse goes. We're a team. I have medical papers that let Tesse travel with me as a support animal. I convinced the doctors I was a bit crazy, so they allowed it."

Actually, the 'crazy' part isn't really so far-fetched for my human partner Ole.

Mr. Fische raised an eyebrow at Ole's comment but decided not to dispute the doctor's diagnosis. "My cab is waiting; I really must toddle along now. We will see you in the morning."

CHAPTER 2

After Mr. Fische left, Ole went to the sink and ran himself a glass of water. "Well, that was certainly interesting wasn't it?"

"Are you sure we aren't sleeping and it was all just a weird dream?" was my answer.

Ole: "There's an empty cup with leftover tea on the table and neither you nor I drink tea so I think it was real."

"You're probably right. The question is, what exactly does all this mean?"

Ole: "Best as I can figure I had a rich relative that left me a lot of money. Just think about it Tesse, we might just be rich. We could eat lobster whenever we want, you could have a diamond studded dog collar and fur booties for your paws during the cold winters."

"Bow-wow…and you could get new vehicles and turn up the heat in the winter so we don't have to depend on that electric blanket to keep us warm on Minnesota's freezing winter nights."

Ole: "Now wait just a minute there. I happen to like the vehicles I have now. I think I'll keep them. No need to be frivolous. However, it would be nice to set the thermostat a few degrees warmer in the winter time. We might even run the air conditioner all day long instead of just on hot nights to help us sleep better. Yup Tesse, looks like our ship has finally come in and it's not on the Mississippi but straight across the North Atlantic from England."

"As long as that ship doesn't have Titanic painted on the bow and the life jackets we should be all right."

Ole: "That was sort of funny but I'm afraid it was in bad taste."

"You're right, I am sorry. That was a totally insensitive thing for me to say."

Ole: "I'm pretty excited about tomorrow. It will be interesting to find out exactly what we inherited."

"It sure will. What should we do now? We need something to take our minds off it."

Ole: "I think we should take a nap. We are about three-quarters of the way through the Railway Detective book by Edward Marston and it would be nice to see what happens next."

"Oh yeah, the bad guys were about to blow up the Liverpool steam locomotive. That sounds like a great idea. You can read it out loud until we get tired and then we can go to sleep. A good sleep for an hour or so should help us calm down and not think about the fortune that awaits us."

Ole: "Don't be counting buffalo chips before they drop, we don't know if there is a fortune or not. Even if there is our dear departed relative might have a pile of debt to go with it."

"Killjoy," was all I had to say to that.

When morning came, Ole made us waffles for breakfast, smothered with syrup and melted butter. He had pineapple-orange juice, and I had my preferred bowl of milk.

"How did you sleep last night?" I asked him.

Ole: "Not so well. I kept thinking about English castles and riches and how it would be to be a nobleman in England. You know what do they call it? One of the landed gentry. Of course I would treat my tenant people just like anyone else. No reason to put on airs as the English might say. What about you old chap, how did you sleep?"

"Pretty much the same except for all the landed gentry crap and considering others as lesser than myself. Doggone-it. I hope if we actually do get something amazing you aren't going to get all 'sticky-wicket' about it mate."

Ole: "What a bunch of idiots we are. I would hope that any amount of money or property doesn't change us at all. The two of us from Yahooville, Minnesota probably wouldn't fit in to well over in jolly old England."

"Well, you best get shaved, showered and put on something other than jeans and a t-shirt so you look presentable to Mr. Fische. When you're finished you can give me a good brushing and spoof me up a bit."

We had a bit of time left before it was time to go, so we went onto the deck and sat quietly, watching the Mississippi flow by. A few squirrels chasing each other around occasionally diverted our attention, as did a crow who nosily seemed to object to us being near his turf.

Ole looked at his watch and said. "Best we get a move on. Don't want to be late. I have a feeling Mr. Fische is a very punctual person and our being a bit early or at least there on the dot would certainly be what he expects and nothing less."

A bit more traffic than we anticipated and hitting one too many of the myriad of stoplights that dotted the roads on our way there had us pulling into the Holiday Inn with three minutes to spare. Mr. Fische was standing by the doorway awaiting our arrival. His briefcase in one hand and his suitcase on the ground at his side. An umbrella was hanging from his arm, as one might expect to see in some old English movie, but not so much in the United States and certainly not in Minnesota. Now if he had a snow shovel in his hand, that would be more normal. Bow-wow…just kidding.

As soon as we had stopped, Ole jumped out of the car and rushed over to grab Mr. Fische's suitcase. Ole put the suitcase in the back of our Honda CRV and then ran to open the front door for Mr. Fische, who was patiently waiting for him. It seems Mr. Fische was used to having others do things for him. I had to wonder if he had a chauffeur back home or if he preferred to sit in the back and treat Ole as a chauffeur. No matter now, I had to ride in the back, which under the circumstances of possible riches, I didn't mind.

Ole: "Good morning Mr. Fische. I trust you had a pleasant evening."

Mr. Fische. "Pleasant enough. I spent a good hour discussing your case with the home office. I am sure you will be pleased to know that they agreed with my assumption that you are the person we have been searching for."

Ole: "That certainly is good news. I hope Mr. Fische that you have had a light breakfast and have saved lots of room for lunch."

Mr. Fische: "Actually I have. I just had a cup of tea and one of your biscuits or as you Americans call them cookies. Of course it was hard to deviate from my normal routine of a hardy breakfast and a light lunch but I am curious to try as many of your Native American dishes as my stomach will hold. I hope you do not mind if I make a glutton of myself."

Ole: "If you want American food I have just the place in mind."

Mr. Fische: "I seldom get excited about anything but I am very much looking forward to this culinary adventure. May I be so bold as to ask the name of the establishment that we will be visiting?"

Ole: "You may. It's called Rollie's Rednecks and Longnecks. It just so happens to be the number-one Honkey-Tonk bar in Minnesota."

Mr. Fische: "I feel you have me at a disadvantage in the meanings of some of your words. Redneck? Longneck? And Honkey-Tonk all have me quite bewildered."

Ole chuckled to himself. I quickly pointed out to my partner that Mr. Fische was a guest on our land. If we went to England, there would probably be lots of words and customs that would bewilder us. So, I told Ole to be patient and explain the meaning of the words to Mr. Fische. Also, I reminded him to be polite about it.

Ole: "I understand your bewilderment Mr. Fische. I'm sure if we were in your country we would also be confused. Not let's see. First off Rollie is the owner and that's his name, He has a country western band that sometimes plays music there. You are familiar with country western music aren't you?"

Mr. Fische: "Vaguely. I have heard songs in some of your western picture shows. The Good, the Bad and the Ugly, that was a rather catchy tune. Oh and one of my favorites, True Grit with John Wayne and the singer Glen Campbell, of course I will overlook the fact that he is Irish. Although I have to admit that many of the Irish have excellent voices and they are a people who love to sing, dance and over indulge in the spirits. "

Ole: "Yes, the Good, the Bad and the Ugly had a catchy tune but it didn't have any words. Glen Campbell singing True Grit is a classic western tune. How about Johnny Cash, Willie Nelson, Dolly Parton or Reba McIntire. Have you heard of any of them?"

Mr. Fische: "Johnny Cash does ring a bell. 'I walk the line' I believe is one of his songs. Would that be country western?"

Ole: "It would. That's the type of music Rollie and his band sing. Plus a few older rock n' roll songs. You are familiar with rock n' roll?"

Mr. Fische: "Of course the English invented it. The Beatles, Herman's Hermits, The Rolling Stones just to name a few."

Ole was tempted to bring up Buddy Holly, Chuck Berry, and Elvis Presley, but I told him it was probably best not to under the circumstances. After all, we were hoping for some big money on this deal, and we wouldn't want to take a chance at offending Mr. Fische.

"Now, what about the rednecks and longnecks. Just what exactly do those words mean?"

Ole: Longnecks is pretty easy to describe. Basically, it refers to a bottle of beer with an elongated neck. Redneck, now that's sort of a tough one. It used to be a negative stereotype associated with the uneducated, ignorant, or possibly a bigot. Recently it seems that the old-fashioned American cowboy types almost wear the name as a badge of pride. They would consider themselves as just good old-fashioned Americans who value common sense and right from wrong as their badge of honor.

Mr. Fische: "May I be so bold as to ask if you consider yourself as one of the rednecks?"

Ole: "That's probably a question I shouldn't answer until after our meeting is finished. I'd hate to think a wrong answer might affect the outcome of our meeting."

Mr. Fische: "Please pardon my indiscretion. The question was totally unprofessional for me to ask. I hope you will forgive me. Of course speaking for our law firm our reputation is spotless and our firm would never let your answer have any effect on the outcome of your inheritance. In fact the matter has already been decided."

Ole: "No problem there Fische ol' chap. I'll give you an answer just to satisfy your curiosity after our meeting is finished."

Oh boy. My Ole just had to slip into the 'redneck good ol' country boy mode every so often. I can't believe he just said 'Fische ol' chap.' Nothing like a little American country boy mixed with some unwarranted English familiarity.

We pulled into Rollie's parking lot, with its corral filled with a herd of full-sized fiberglass longhorn cattle located behind the bar. A huge American flag fluttered from the pole at the front of the building. A replica General Lee Dodge Charger took a prominent parking spot near the entrance as a large full-sized fiberglass boar sat guarding the entrance. A motorcycle and pickup truck sat high up on thirty-foot poles at the parking lot's perimeter. A special area was set aside for motorcycle parking with a hitching rail on the boardwalk just in case you rode in on a horse. A replica of 'Tater,' the tow truck, peaked from around the far corner of the building. Pepsi products were advertised in big, bold letters on the door as Coca-Cola had sort of boycotted itself as a 'redneck' beverage.

We entered into the slightly dark old-time saloon atmosphere. A long bar predominantly ran along the wall with a myriad of advertising in neon lights for assorted beers. An old motorcycle, a kiddie car, and lots of country band memorabilia decorated the walls. Mannequins of Elvis Presley and Willie Nelson were sitting at a table in a back corner.

Ole offered to lead the way past the dance floor and the bandstand to an unoccupied booth in a somewhat secluded, quiet spot for our meeting. Mr. Fische almost bumped into a few tables and even some of the patrons as he took in an overload of sights and sounds of a real honest-to-goodness honky-tonk bar.

Mr. Fische: "It sort of reminds me of some of the old-time village pubs in my own country. A bit dark inside, and a smell of ale and the working class in the air. I must say I was pleased to see three gentlemen at the bar wearing cowboy hats. I even noticed that two of them had six shooters holstered on their belts. Now I can return to England and tell everyone that I saw some honest-to-goodness American cowboys.

Ole decided not to burst Mr. Fische's observation. The men did have on cowboy hats, although there are not very many dyed-in-the-wool real cowboys in central Minnesota. As for the guns, Minnesota has a permit-to-carry law, and those six shooters were most likely Glock 9mm handguns which are lightweight and provide a pretty good punch if you are shot by one. For now, it was best to leave Mr. Fische with the dream he had of seeing real cowboys.

If we ever went to England, we would have the same type of hope and dreams of seeing the Queen or meeting real English people who hung out in pubs and played darts while drinking pints of warm beer. If we could spend a night in a castle or rent a thatch-roofed cottage, it would make all our dreams of England come true. Meeting other aristocracy would probably not be at the top of our list. Then again, we have no desire to meet the current president of our own country, and very few of our countries celebrate, and not any of the sports figures. We would make an exception for Bruce Campbell, Tim Allen, Elvira, or Willie Nelson.

We had just settled into our booth when a waitress in tight blue jeans with sequined designs on the back pockets and a red and white checkered shirt appeared to take our drink order. She smiled at Mr. Fische and commented that she liked his bowler hat. He quickly removed it from his head and set it next to him on the bench seat as he profusely apologized for his bad manners at not having removed it sooner in the presence of a lady or even why he had not removed it as soon as he entered this fine establishment. I guess all the baseball cap-wearing customers and the three cowboys could take a lesson on etiquette from our overseas visitor.

Just a side note. Ole seldom wears hats; he's afraid they might smother his full head of now-greying hair. However, when we vacation out west in the Dakota and Wyoming, he does wear his worn old cowboy hat.

The waitress was amused by Mr. Fische's embarrassment, so she did her best to make him feel more comfortable as she said. "Why that's all right honey, it's nice to have a real gentleman in here that has some manners. What would you gentlemen like to drink? Ole, I assume you and Tesse are having your usual? As for your friend, what would you like, sir? We have all the name brands of beer on tap, or maybe you would prefer a mixed drink or cocktail."

Cocktail, come on, she had to be kidding?

Ole: "We'll have our usual."

Waitress: "Sir, what can I get for you?"

Mr. Fische: "Mister Ole, what is your usual?"

Ole: "It's a local drink invented by a dear old friend of mine. It's called SvenBrew beer and it's brewed near here at the Cold Spring Brewery."

Mr. Fische: "Does it come in one of those long-neck bottles?"

Waitress: "It does, or we also have it on tap. Ole likes his on tap in a twenty ounce glass with three green olives. Tesse prefers hers in a bowl, no olives."

Mr. Fische: "I do believe I would like to try a SvenBrew beer in a long-neck bottle. Would it be inappropriate for me to keep the empty bottle as a souvenir?"

Waitress: "Inappropriate? Not at all, the bottles are non-returnable so we just toss them into the trash when they are empty for recycling. If you want to take some home to your friends I'll find some empties for you and rinse them out."

Mr. Fische: "I may have more than one and if you could rinse my empty ones out for me I would be very grateful."

The waitress toddled off, as the English might say to get our drinks as we looked over the menu. Mr. Fische had spent only a brief time pondering his choices when a smile came to his face.

Mr. Fische: "I see on the menu a 'cowboy burger' topped with onion rings, Swiss cheese, barbeque sauce and pickles. Would that be a good choice for real genuine American cuisine?"

Ole: "It would. Add a side of deep fried cheese curds and your meal will be really American."

Mr. Fische: "Good. Now that I've made my decision on what to eat let's get to down to business."

Mr. Fische put his briefcase on the seat next to him. He opened it and proceeded to pull out a stack of papers which he laid on the table before him. He briefly checked them over to make sure they were all in order before he started talking. Ole and I sat with bated breath listening for what he had to say.

Mr. Fische: "After a lengthy telephone call to my partner last night we have come to a decision that you are the sole beneficiary to your great-grandfathers will. I have copies of all the legal details for you. It would take quite a few hours for you to read through and digest everything that is written here so if you wish I can give you a condensed version verbally which will cover the high points. Then I will leave copies with you to read at your leisure."

Ole looked at the stack of papers he had just been handed, and then he looked at me. I shrugged my ears and told him to accept the condensed verbal version for now, and we could read the rest later.

Mr. Fische: "To put it in simplified terms you are the prime and only individual named in your great-grandfather's will. There are to the best of our knowledge no other living relatives or individuals that could contest the contents or the intent of your great-grandfathers estate. As the sole solicitors of Fische & Chipps being the legal representatives for your great-grandfather and his estate I am proud to announce that after extensive research that we have found you to be the one and only heir to your great-grandfathers estate, holdings and finances. Do you have any questions so far?"

Questions? Was he crazy or just enjoying keeping us in suspense?

Ole: "Well, Fischey old chap. Not to be rude but give it to us short and sweet. What exactly are we inheriting?"

There he goes again, getting a bit too chummy with the man who is about to give us a fortune.

Mr. Fische: "To give you a brief history as to why and how the scope of these holdings are so vast, you need to go back to the time of the Viking raiders sometime between 800 to 1150 AD. It seems that one of your forebearers brokered a peace between the Viking raiders and Alfred the Great of England in what became known as Longhall County in England. This county got its name from the marriage union between the Long family of England and the Hall family of Germany. This peace treaty so impressed Alfred that he granted the land to the Long and Hall dynasty. To this very day, the county of Longhall has been owned lock, stock, and barrel by what was believed to be the last surviving member, your great-grandfather, and now you. It includes not only all the lands in Longhall County but also the village of Hedgehoghaven, located in said county. Also included is the Hedgehoghaven Railway, with its connecting lines to the major rail lines of England. The original Castle of Longhall is unfortunately now in ruins on top of Longhall Mountain. For the last hundred years or so, the Longhall family has resided in the Poachers Rest at the base of Longhall Mountain. Of course, there is also a very substantial amount of money and assets associated with your inheritance, and with the way your great-grandfather and we arranged his will, the taxes going to the government have been kept to a minimum so that you will be able to live out your days as a gentleman of leisure. If you accept the terms of the will, you will also inherit the title of 'Lord'. So in your case, your proper title will be 'Lord Ole'.

'Lord Ole.' Now I've heard it all. It's one thing to inherit land, property, or money. But to inherit a title. It's just so, well, you know, so British.

Our food arrived, and at the sight of it, Mr. Fische quickly gathered up all the papers on the table and slipped them back into his briefcase. His eyes were the size of saucers and made to look even larger from the magnification of his eyeglasses as he looked at his cowboy burger with its bit of grease seeping out along the edge of the beef patty and dripping onto the plate. He slipped the mighty cowboy-sized burger into both his hands and found he could barely get his mouth around it to take a bite.

Ole: "I take it our business is on hold for the time being?"

Mr. Fische: "It is. This may not be tea time in England but its close enough. When tea time comes around the world of business stops. I cannot imagine letting this scrumptious cowboy burger getting cold. I must admit I have never seen a burger of such huge proportions."

He then took a swig of SvenBrew right from the bottle and savored its flavor before swallowing. Next came the cheese curds dipped in Mariana sauce, more beer, more burgers, and more cheese curds. Well, you get the picture.

Ole: "Rollie's takes pride in making sure his meals are large enough to satisfy the working class. Cowboys of course are hard workers and they expect a substantial meal to fill them up and hold them over until their next meal comes along. Also, this just so happens to be Rollie's place and one thing he believes in besides America is large hefty portions of food."

Ole had ordered a cowboy pizza for us. Flame-cooked with chicken, onion rings, and barbeque sauce topping. As Mr. Fische continued to savor his burger and cheese curds, he was also eyeing up our pizza.

Mr. Fische: "I must say these deep fried cheese curds are every bit as taster if not better than the chips we get with our fish back home. I wonder if it would be proper for me to ask if I might try a slice of that cowboy pizza of yours."

Ole: "Pizza is made to be shared with friends. Help yourself."

Mr. Fische: "That is most gracious of you. I never realized that cowboys ate pizza. I always imagined it as more of an Italian cuisine."

Ole: "America has always been a melting pot of cultures and we tend to take what we like and make it our own. Cowboy pizza is certainly a prime example and I'm not sure if it exists anywhere else other than Rollie's."

Mr. Fische: "It is very different. Quite tasty actually. Every bit as good as my cowboy burger and cheese curds. As for the SvenBrew beer I note a bit of raspberry and strawberry flavor, also quite pleasing to the palette I might add."

He missed the best ingredient to SvenBrew. Besides raspberry and strawberry, it also has a puppy dog's kiss.

For being a rather small fellow, Mr. Fische managed to pack away everything on his plate, plus three pieces of pizza and three SvenBrews.

Once we had finished our meals, Mr. Fische excused himself to go to the 'wc'.

I, of course, had to ask what the heck a 'wc.' is

Ole: "Best I can recall from watching lots of British movies it's a 'water closet'. One of their words for a bathroom or restroom, I think they also sometimes call it the 'loo'."

All I could say was that I sure was glad we lived in America, where I understood the language.

Ole: "You do know most of our language originated from England when we were still considered their colonies until after the Revolutionary War."

I looked at Ole and said. "I'm happy with American English. I think I'll let the British keep their English to themselves."

Ole: "If we actually inherit an estate in England and become a 'Lord' we might have to adapt and learn some of their sayings.

Mr. Fische returned and quickly got back to business. The waitress had cleared our table, so he had a large clean area to spread out his paperwork.

Mr. Fische: "Time for us to finish up our business here. If you would like to read this one particular document and sign and date it I can begin the process of transferring your great-grandfathers estate and holdings into your name on my return to London."

Ole looked over the document. It was only a half dozen paragraphs detailing things about Longhall County, the village of Hedgehoghaven, Hedgehoghaven Railway, and the Poachers Rest cottage, all waiting for the process of being transferred to Ole. Ole read on intently until the last paragraph, which stopped him dead in his tracks.

Ole: "Everything looks fine up until the last paragraph. If I read that paragraph correctly it states that for me to be eligible to accept the inheritance that I need to move to England and take up residence at the Poachers Rest cottage. Is that correct?"

Mr. Fische: "Partially correct. You will need to take up 'permanent' residence in the County of Longhall. So you must find permanent residence in the County. The Poachers Rest has been in your family for some time, starting in the 1700s when Longhall Castle fell into disrepair and is now just a pile of ruins. The castle is slowly crumbling away, and even when it was livable, it was much too cold and damp to be comfortable. By that time, the family was down to only a few members and no longer required such a large residence, so it was decided to take over the Poachers Rest when the current owner had passed away. It was used as a boarding house and tavern, so there was more than enough room for the family and a few servants.

The Poachers Rest is built nestled into a corner of Longhall Mountain, not far from the castle. A railway track is near the front door. Your great-grandfather did not care much for driving or for automobiles. So he had a 0-4-0 Hedgehoghaven locomotive, and a private railway coach that would pick him up at the door of the Poachers Rest and take him to one of the two passenger stations at the village of Hedgehoghaven or drop him off from one of the two mainlines that run near the village depending on where he wanted to go. Since your great-grandfathers passing the spur line is now being used mostly for a nearby mine just west of the Poachers Rest,

If you do not find the current residence to your liking, that part of the will is negotiable. You are moving to England, and taking up residence somewhere in Longhall County is not negotiable. If you refuse the inheritance, it will be confiscated and taken over by the United Kingdom. Not something the residents of Longhall County and the Village of Hedgehoghaven would be in favor of. They may not know you, but certainly, they would consider you the lesser of two evils as the owner and Lord of Longhall County."

Ole: "Moving to England is a pretty big step. I think Tesse and I may have to think this one over a bit."

Mr. Fische: "I think it might be best if you would take me to the airport now. You can never be too early to catch a flight in this day and age. You have twenty-four hours to give us your answer about accepting all the conditions of the will and moving to England. If the answer is no the estate will become the property of the government, that would be a sad state of affairs indeed. If the answer is yes I can give you 48 hours to arrive in England and take over the estate. I'll call you tomorrow about this time for your answer."

On our way to the airport, Ole asked a very important question. "Mr. Fische, I am not a wealthy man. Just how am I supposed to make a living if I decide to move to England?"

Mr. Fische: "You may have missed one of the provisions of the will that we talked about. If you move to England, you will actually be quite wealthy. Not only from the money and investments your great-grandfather has left you. You also own the whole of Longhall County, which includes the village and railway of Hedgehoghaven. There is no private ownership in the whole county. Every building, farm, and home is owned by you.

The residents pay rent which covers all the expenses and upkeep for the county and also pay for any taxes required by the government, which are minimal as the arrangement with King Alfred put a cap on what the government could charge, and that has no time limit, much to the digress of the United Kingdom.

Another nice source of revenue comes from the freight and passenger service provided by the railway. The whole thing is a rather archaic feudal-style arrangement that was set up hundreds of years ago by your forebearers. The cost to the residents has been kept at a minimum, and it is much cheaper for them to live this way than in any other place in the United Kingdom. Most have long-term leases, some of them up to ninety-nine years, so that not only do they not have to worry about being evicted, they can plan on their children taking over their businesses, farms, or homes if they want to."

Ole: "Tesse and I will have an answer for you tomorrow. By the way people would probably consider me a redneck."

CHAPTER 3

Our ride home was pretty quiet. Here we were on the verge of a huge inheritance with lots of money and land within our grasp. The only thing was we would have to leave the security of everything we now had. Our home, our friends, oops, scratch that last part, we really don't have any friends. With the political climate and the liberals forcing us to accept their cockamamie, no common sense ideas, and the few people we talk to are just scary as they lean to the left or the right. We couldn't agree that the legal killing of unborn babies is all right. Or if you don't wear a mask, you can lose your job or the ability to travel. It was almost like a Nazi-style government was taking over the United States, except maybe Florida, Texas, or South Dakota. The only problem was that we lived in Minnesota, considered a 'blue' state which we associate with 'blue' as being icy cold to any kind of common sense. If only there was a common sense political party that used their brain and the God-given ten commandants as a basis for decisions or did things for the majority of the people instead of the minority, as Ole was taught when he went to school. All right, my political tirade is over for now; back to what Ole and I should do. Stay here and join the vaccinated 'Nazi' part so we can keep our jobs and travel as we want to, or go to England and live in Longhall County, where the people would be allowed to make decisions that would benefit the majority of those that would be living under our domain.

We arrived home, and to get us in the mood for the discussion that we both knew we had to have, Ole made himself hot cocoa and warm milk for me. Then we lay on the bed, and I listened as Ole read two chapters from the fifth book in the Railway Detective series called *The Brighton Express* by Edward Marston. A good reading choice for the moment as it deals with old-fashioned England and with trains. After two chapters had been read, we both took a cat nap. Oops, the 'cat' reference didn't mean for that to slip in.

After our nap, Ole took some venison chili out of the refrigerator and heated up a bowl for each of us, with a generous sprinkling of cheese curds on top of the hot chili and a bottle of Squirt for himself, and a bowl of water for me we went to our basement theater room to watch reruns of Last Man Standing with Tim Allen.

After we had watched episode two, Ole finally shut the television off and spoke up.

Ole: "Well Tesse. We don't have much time to think about Mr. Fische's proposal. What's your take on moving to England and collecting our inheritance?"

"You keep saying you're getting older and this isn't the America you grew up in. It's your inheritance and it's up to you if you want to accept it and move to England. As for me. I'm your partner and I'll do whatever you want to do. From the way Mr. Fische made it sound Longhall County is sort of a world apart from the current control of England, sort of a fiefdom and you would be like its king."

Ole: "Last thing I would want is to be a king. In fact you might have just helped me make up my mind. Here we are living under that dictator President in the United States. He wants to control our vaccinations, have us report to the government every time we deposit $600 or more in our bank accounts and curb our freedom of speech so basically we are like a dog being muzzled. If we go to England and I can have a major say to run a county where freedom is paramount and you can say what you think and run your business as you see best as long as it doesn't hurt anyone else I say let's do it."

"What if what you say or how you run your business offends someone?"

Ole: "If someone says something that offends me I either blow it off as ignorance on their part or I might try to discuss the problem with them. If I get really pissed I'll keep my mouth shut and just eliminate them from my life or if that's not possible have as minimal of contact with them as possible."

"What about controlling crime or protesters?"

Ole: "Hopefully the village has law enforcement to deal with crime. As for protesters, if they are peaceful let them be, otherwise call in law enforcement."

"I think you'll make a great king. Of course I do hope you will crack down on any free roving felines that might be in your county."

We both laughed at that one. However, I was sort of serious. Free-roaming cats upsetting garbage cans, pooping in kids' sandboxes, and meowing all night are a public nuisance in my mind.

Ole: "That's it. My mind is made up. We'll find someone we can trust to move in here. Probably one of my kids. I'll call Mr. Fische in the morning and have him make arrangements for us to go to England."

"What about me. Do you think they will quarantine me? I here they do that to dogs that travel abroad."

Ole: "I'll explain to Mr. Fische that you just had a complete physical and all your shots are up to date. I've got papers saying you are a service dog assigned to me and that you can travel by air with me. Maybe with that information he can get an exemption to keep you from being quarantined."

"I sure hope so. Last thing I want is to be locked up in a cage for two weeks or more."

First thing in the morning, Ole made a phone call to Mr. Fische, and arrangements were made for us to fly to England. Mr. Fische had taken the initiative to have a reservation already on hold for us, and he had even started the process of getting me into England without having to go through the quarantine process. All we had to do was to call my veterinarian and have him email all the relevant medical records and paperwork to the office of Fische & Chipps Solicitors.

In a whirlwind of making phone calls packing up the bare minimum of luggage, and locating copies of medical records, service dog status, and Ole's passport, we were soon in a cab and on our way to the airport.

We flew from our local airport to the Minneapolis-St. Paul terminal, then on to Chicago, and then straight through to England. After eleven hours of Ole with leg cramps and a bad backache, we landed in London, England.

As we made our way through the busy airport terminal, I did my best to avoid being stepped on, bumped into, and getting petted by little kids and even a few adults. Ole did his best to point out my 'service dog' jacket, which to those in the know, meant to leave me alone and let me do my job. To speed things along, Ole finally set me on top of his roller luggage, and I at least got to ride in comfort for about half our journey to the outside of the terminal and into the fresh air.

Once we had left the airport's restricted area, we stepped outside to a cloudy, drizzled, soaked sidewalk bustling with taxis and limousines waiting for their customers. We were told by Mr. Fische that someone would be there to pick us up and take us to the solicitor's office. Ole glanced around at the assorted taxis and limos, and then to our surprise, he noticed a Mercedes limousine with an immaculate black-suited man with a limo driver's cap holding up a sign that said Ole & Tesse. We hurried over with our one piece of rolling wheeled luggage, with me being jostled about as I rode on top of it. The limo driver quickly grabbed me and put me in the back seat as he held the door open for Ole to enter. He tossed our luggage into the trunk as we settled in for our ride.

Once the driver was back in the car and we had started moving, he introduced himself with a British accent that both Ole and I found a bit difficult to understand as he most likely found our American accent rather hard to comprehend. He introduced himself as 'David' and asked if we would like for him to give us a running commentary of the sights we would see as we drove through London. Of course, Ole said yes, and I gave a 'bark' yes myself, and it was very interesting even though we only understood about half of what he said.

Once we arrived at the offices of Fische & Chipps, David opened our car door and escorted us to the entrance of the building. He said he would be waiting for us when we finished our business and then he would take us to the train station.

We entered the building and were greeted by a very prim and proper receptionist dressed in a conservative grey jacket and skirt ensemble. She looked at Ole, who was dressed in black jeans and a button-down dress shirt. Then she looked at me in my service dog coat and smiled.

Receptionist: "You must be Mister Ole and Tesse. Mr. Fische is expecting you. I'll let him know you are here. Please have a seat; it should only take a few minutes before he can see you. I'll get some tea ready for your meeting.

Within a short while, we were escorted to Mr. Fische's office. The room was much smaller than we expected. It was crowded with bookshelves filled with law books, his desk and chair took up a great deal of space, and the two chairs across from his desk came close to filling up the room. He invited us to sit down just as the receptionist came in with tea and cookies for Mr. Fische and Ole. She brought me a bowl of water and no treats. Ole, of course, shared his cookies with me to a rather surprised look from the receptionist. I was proud to see Ole acting polite as he drank his tea without complaining, even though he really didn't care much for it.

Of course, Mr. Fische had seen me eating at the booth at Rollie's Rednecks and Longnecks, so he was used to how Ole treated me as his partner and not as a pet.

Mr. Fische was in his element and was all business. He explained the fine points of each paper from the huge pile on his desk and how each pertained to the inheritance we were about to commit to in full, with the understanding that our lives would now be tied irrevocably and forever to our new ownership of Longhall County and everything associated and contained within it for the rest of our lives. A very scary concept, to say the least.

Ole was just about to sign the papers when he stopped. Mr. Fische had a worried look in his eyes. If we didn't sign, everything would become the property of England, and Mr. Fische would be out of a job as far as being the solicitor for not only us but for all of Longhall County. Of course, one would have to assume this was a very tidy sum in the coin of the realm, which, as we understood it, would be in English pounds and not American dollars.

Mr. Fische: "Is there a problem Mister Ole."

Ole: "Actually there is. I understand that I need to be a permanent resident in Longhall County. I think that in the long run I may become rather bored just sitting around being called 'Lord' with nothing to do. It seems you have been doing most of the legal work and keeping the books which as far as I can see is not something I would want to change. What would happen if I wanted to operate my own business in Hedgehoghaven providing a building would be open for me to do so? Also, would Tesse and I be able to take a vacation back to the United States for say two to four weeks at a time?"

Mr. Fische: "Mr. Chipps and I would be very grateful to remain as your solicitors and we will send you an itemized statement every month as to the collections and disbursements for your holdings. As far as taking a holiday or as you Americans call it a 'vacation' there is nothing in the contract that would restrict you from traveling as long as it is not more than six-weeks during a one calendar year period."

Ole looked at me, and I nodded my head in agreement. After all, he is my human, and what he wanted, I wanted. Who knows, maybe Longhall County would prove to be a nice place to live. Leaving our old hometown seemed so much easier as daily violence was becoming a more commonplace experience. We could only hope our new home would be more like the America Ole grew up in. He liked the old days of knowing almost everyone in his town and the way they helped and looked after each other. That's the way we both wanted to live.

Ole finally signed the papers and officially ended our old way of life. He thanked Mr. Fische, and we went back to the Limo to be delivered to the train station, which to our surprise, was almost as busy as a Washington DC subway. By the way, Ole had been on the subway and didn't much care for the crowds. Mr. Fische supplied us with tickets for the train and the coin of the realm for us to pay any expenses that may arise on our way to our new home. We would have to make two transfers before we would board the Hedgehoghaven train that would take us to our final destination.

CHAPTER 4

Ole being a dyed-in-the-wool train enthusiast, was a bit disappointed by the British Rail Class 254 locomotive that delivered us to the first leg of our destination. Not that there was anything wrong with the locomotive. It was a design from the 1970s and still did a good job today. He just wasn't thrilled by the new sleek designs and modern modes of rail transportation. He felt the same way when he traveled by Amtrak in the United States.

I told him the past was the past, and the present did not lend itself to travel by steam locomotives in this day and age. Of course, there were railway enthusiasts who kept some of the old steam locomotives operating for people like themselves and for tourists. However, one had to wonder how long they could keep it up with the new generation screaming for an end to pollution and a push to electrify everything that moved.

Of course, none of them had enough common sense to realize that all those batteries that ran this new dream machinery of theirs needed natural resources to be mined and produced to operate their dream machines. They also seemed to ignore the issue of how to dispose of the waste when their vehicles and batteries reached the end of their life. At this time, it looks as if just the replacement of a battery that operates the vehicle may be more than the vehicle is worth, so off to the scrap yard goes the whole shebang. Ole, of course, was still driving a 2003 Honda CRV when we left home, 20 years old and running like the day it was new with a bare minimum of repairs and probably another ten years of life in it.

We studied the train schedule board to no avail. There were times for arrival and departures and which track to be on and which train to board for all sorts of towns and places around England, but there was nothing that even remotely hinted of any connection to Hedgehoghaven.

We finally managed to find a railway employee and asked if she could give us directions on where to board a train to the Village of Hedgehoghaven. She asked to see our ticket, and she chuckled as she handed it back to us.

Employee: "You really are going to the Village of Hedgehoghaven? From your accent, I assume you are a Yank. It figures. I suppose you came to England to see a quaint old English village to visit. If that's the case, you chose the right place. The Village of Hedgehoghaven is still living in the past, and modern-day amenities don't exist there. Won't be any five-star hotels or fancy eating places there. It's not too late to change your mind. You can always trade that ticket in for someplace more modern and up-to-date.

Ole: "No changing our minds. That's where we want to go. We own a cottage there."

She laughed out loud as she said. "You Yanks are a gullible bunch. So someone sold you a cottage there. I suppose they told you how quaint and picturesque it is there and it might just be so. The folks that live there can be a mighty quirky lot. You wait and see, I give you a week and you'll be high tailing it back to the colonies."

Ole: "Maybe so, maybe not. We plan on staying for a long time. Would you please just give us directions as to where we can catch the next train that will get us there?"

Employee: "Of course. You go behind this station and walk the tracks about a quarter of a kilometer until you come to a little run-down brick building with a few benches and a loo inside. There will be a sign that says Hedgehoghaven Station.

The train to there is run by the Hedgehoghaven Railway, and it only comes here once a week for goods and occasional passengers. The schedule is not very regular. Usually, the train should show up between noon and 4 pm. Of course, that is if it doesn't break down. If that happens, it might be midnight before you see it. Don't worry, though. It always shows up sometimes on the day it's supposed to. It may take an hour or two after it arrives before it leaves as it usually brings some empty wagons and exchanges them for full ones. That's the main way they get supplies to their village. Only one road goes there, and it's a single-lane and not well-kept, so vehicle traffic is pretty sparse. I wish you luck. You'll need it."

We went behind the main station, and unlike the multiple tracks and crowds of people, we were greeted by a rusty set of rails and a hard-packed dirt path that was slowly being taken over by weeds. We walked along the path until we came to the brick building that had been described to us. We looked at the well-weathered sign hanging loosely from the eve of the building by a single hook on the one edge as the other side had come loose from age. The paint on the sign was faded but legible, and it said Hedgehoghaven Station.

We opened the door with a bit of a push as the hinges were rusted and groaned at being opened. Inside the room were two rows of green-painted benches with the paint peeling off. Ole made a close inspection of the benches to make sure they were still sturdy enough to hold our weight before we sat down. A rusted water fountain looked as if it was probably not safe to drink from, and a candy vending machine half full of nasty-looking candy bars sat along one wall. A coin-operated postcard vending machine was near the bathroom, and it had two columns of postcards. One was a picture of a steam locomotive pulling passenger coaches at a picturesque railway station with the Hedgehoghaven name on it. The other postcard was of a quaint village with the Hedgehoghaven name below it. The two main buildings in the village postcard seemed to be a place called Chaps Pub and Kelley's Arcade. Just for fun and as a souvenir, Ole bought both of the postcards.

Ole made a quick trip to the room marked 'WC" as we had learned from Mr. Fische was the 'water closet' or the loo, as the station agent told us to use the bathroom. Then we sat and waited. There were a couple of magazines from the 1990s laying on the bench, so Ole and I looked at them and waited.

I was the first to hear it, and I nudged Ole and told him to listen. Slowly the sound of a chugging steam locomotive could be heard, and it was getting closer. Both of us left our seats and went outside to stand on the platform waiting in anticipation of maybe getting to see a real steam locomotive. Possibly it was a tourist train or a vintage locomotive being moved during restoration.

Ole picked me up so I could see better as he pointed down the tracks. Off in the distance, small puffs of smoke wafted into the air. Ole's dream of seeing a live steam locomotive in England looked to be coming true. I, for one, was excited more for him than me. Then again, seeing an operating steam locomotive in this day and age was a rare and unusual occurrence.

The last time we saw one was back home in 2020 in Duluth, Minnesota, when the Union Pacific 4-8-8-4 Big Boy was making its tour of the United States. It was like seeing a living smoke-breathing dragon come to life.

Ole became even more excited as the front of an actual steam locomotive came into view, and it was on the very track we were standing next to. He quickly put me down and pulled out his cell phone, ready to start taking a video as the train came past us. However, amazingly as the locomotive came closer, it began to slow down. Ole hollered in excitement to me that the locomotive was pulling a vintage four-wheeled passenger coach and some four-wheeled goods wagons, and it looked like it might just be the train from Hedgehoghaven.

But wait, the train came to a stop before it reached us. A man jumped down from the brake van and uncoupled the goods wagons from the brake van. The train then proceeded forward until it cleared a switch and then shunted the goods wagons onto a siding. The goods wagons were uncoupled from the passenger coach, which was located right behind the engine. The locomotive and passenger coach then proceeded to move forward and then backed onto another siding to pick up four loaded wagons. Finally, after all the switching was completed, the train was reassembled with the brake van so that it was made up of a crimson-colored Precedent Class 2-4-0 that had been commandeered from the LNWR for service on this train, followed by the four-wheeled passenger coach, four goods wagons and a brake van. All the while, Ole was busy taking pictures and short videos of the operation. He was, to say the least, in seventh heaven.

We were now some distance from the station, so we started walking back as Ole kept mumbling to himself about the marvelous stroke of luck we had just had seeing an actual steam locomotive shuttling its cargo of vintage goods wagons. Of course, we both had to wonder just what was going on. This really didn't seem possible in this day and age as tourist lines usually move just tourists and rail enthusiasts. Stranger still, this was all happening adjacent to a busy mainline passenger station with trains going to and fro to all of England and the rest of the United Kingdom.

We returned to the station, and then we watched as the little 2-4-0 strained a bit to get its load moving. Once it did, it advanced and stopped the passenger coach just a few feet from us.

The engineer stepped off the locomotive and approached us. The fireman stayed with the locomotive, and the brakeman was walking towards us from the back of the train. The engineer wiped his hand on his pants and then held it out for Ole to shake hands.

Engineer: "Mornin' sir. I'm Casey part time engineer of the Hedgehoghaven Railway and full time owner of Chaps Pub of Hedgehoghaven Village. I assume your Ole and this pretty little lady dog is none other than Tesse. Mr. Fische give me a call and told us to pick you up."

Ole: "Sounds like you already know us. Nice to meet you. Is this the normal makeup of the Hedgehoghaven Railway? I mean a steam locomotive and a vintage coach and wagons?"

Casey: "It is. There's lots more back at the train yards. Old Lord Arron was not much of a man for change. He liked the old ways and steam and four wheel wagons he said were good enough for his younger days and they are just as good for today as they was back then.

Hopefully you'll feel the same once you get settled in. You'll find the folks of Hedgehoghaven are not much for change."

Before Ole could say anything, the brakeman was shaking Ole's hand and patting my head as he introduced himself as Captain Pierce. Casey had returned to his locomotive and was busy making preparations for our trip to Hedgehoghaven.

Pierce: "Welcome to the Hedgehoghaven Express. If you would please enter our first-class coach for the journey to our humble village. You will notice that we have a nicely stocked bar and comfortable seating for your journey. It's a bit of a luxury that we stole from watching the movie The Titfield Thunderbolt. Lord Aaron liked his occasional drink, and he felt the passengers would enjoy a bit of the ol' brew as they made the trip from our little world to the hustle and bustle of the new age or vis-versa, as for me just seeing this modern world makes me thirsty to forget it. By the way I'll be your host on this trip. A number of us villagers take turns helping out on the railway as our village can't really afford to hire full-time train crews.

Ole: "What about the brake van. Who's watching that if you're here in the passenger coach?"

Pierce: "No need to worry. Railway regulations require it but we just run slow speed short trains and no major grades on the line. There is really no need for a brake van except to keep the government happy."

The three of us settled in for our trip. Pierce had a mixed drink while Ole settled for a bottle of Squirt soda, and I had a bowl of water. The train was on the move, and we were enjoying the beautiful scenery of England.

Ole: "May I ask why they call you Captain Pierce? Were you in the Navy?"

Pierce: "For a time I was in the Royal Air Force. Ground crew you know. Never flew a plane but I worked on a lot of them. When I left the service I bought me a puffer ship named the Carolsea. Now that old girl, she saw her some service in both the great wars one and two. She was not a fightin' ship mind you but she did coast duty and hauled supplies and coal. That's just as important as any fighting ship. She kept the home front supplied with the goods needed to keep up the fight. Not many of the ol' puffers left but she's one of the best and I plan to keep her that way until the day I die. Then if God wishes she'll keep going under a new master. She's a mighty fine vessel. Once you get settled in you'll have to make a voyage with us."

Ole: "That sounds like a fine idea."

We left the city behind us and were soon traveling through the countryside. Open fields with outcroppings of stone and sheep and cows dotting the fields surrounded by fences of stacked stone that were a marvel of human ingenuity. We went over a stone viaduct and watched the stream below meander along its way. The countryside was green, much like Minnesota in the springtime. The houses and most of the buildings were built of stone or brick, unlike the wooden, vinyl, or steel-sided buildings that were so prevalent where we came from. Pierce didn't say much as he seemed to appreciate that we were enjoying the scenery, and he left us to our thoughts.

The train began to slow down as Captain Pierce announced the 'next stop' Hedgehoghaven Station. We saw a building shaped like a large giant white bulldog as we neared our stop. It looked like some sort of restaurant. The train glided to a smooth stop in front of the yellow-stone Hedgehoghaven Station, which was bustling with a number of passengers and railway employees. Of course, we had to wonder why the station was so busy when no passengers had been dropped off where we had been picked up. We would later learn that some of the main passenger trains from across the British Isles did make a stop at Hedgehoghaven for pick-ups and transfers to different stations.

Tesse: "Did you see that?"

Ole: "See what?"

Tesse: "Paddington Bear."

Ole: "What? Paddington Bear? Are you crazy? He's not real."

Tesse: "He's gone. I swear he was there just a minute ago."

Pierce interrupted our little discussion. "We're here. You can get off at the station and look around a bit or if you wish you can stay here in the car and we'll shunt you over to the mine spur and the Hedgehoghaven 0-4-0 pug engine will take you over to your new home at the Poachers Rest in which case you'll be able to step off this coach right in front of your front door. By the way Casey and I have been sworn to secrecy about who you are so when you are ready to make a formal announcement you can."

Ole was more excited about the pug locomotive than seeing the town, so we, of course, chose the latter of our two options. It would also be nice to see our new home and start settling in.

Once our coach was on the siding, it was only a short time before we heard the little 0-4-0 pug coming along the track. We felt the coach bump as the diminutive little locomotive connected to the coach and pushed us forward. Ole was dying to see the pug and get some pictures, but that would have to wait until we stopped moving.

As we slowly went along, we passed the railway shops. Two large engine sheds, a water tower, coaling bin, a yardmaster's office, and a small stone shed were visible, along with a number of workers going about their duties. Ole couldn't take pictures fast enough as he spied a 4-4-0 locomotive on an outside storage track. The locomotives in the sheds were not too visible, just the rear tender of one and a glimpse of the front of the boiler on the other. I almost had to restrain Ole from jumping out of our coach to see the wonders of steam-age locomotion that were hidden from our sight in those sheds.

Although the village was to the south of us, what caught our attention was a group of men in a grove of trees to the north of us and not far from the railroad yard. One man was sitting on a wooden barrel playing a harmonica. Another man was dancing by himself to the music with a bottle in hand. A campfire was burning, and one of the men was cooking something on a stick as the other two men there were just loitering about. All of them seemed to be enjoying the contents of assorted jugs and bottles that were lying about the area.

We were enjoying the antics of this little show when it abruptly slipped from our sight, and we were now looking straight into a mountain wall. Our coach continued on as we viewed a mining operation that seemed to be in full swing with workers busy with their duties. Then the ruins of a castle came into view. This we knew must be the original Longhall Castle that Mr. Fische had told us about. Even in the daylight, it had an eerie, abandoned look about it.

We could hear the pug slow down, and then we came to a stop. We got out of our seats and headed to the door of the coach. As we stepped down, we were once again greeted by Captain Pierce. "Here you are, home sweet home. Unfortunately, the place has been empty for some time, and all the servants were dismissed after Lord Long passed away. I do believe it has been stocked up with some foodstuff to hold you over for a bit. If you need anything feel free to ring Chaps Pub. Casey is the publican there and will make sure to help you with whatever you need. As for me, I best be toddling along. I'm not only your host, but I am also the engineer of the pug at the moment.

Ole, of course, was torn between trying to take pictures of the departing pug locomotive and checking out our new home. He managed to get a few shots of the pug as it steamed away with our single coach in tow. Then he reverted back to the task at hand, which was admiring our new English home. The Poachers Rest.

In our eyes, this place was the most beautiful example of an English home we could have ever hoped for. The white stucco front with wood timbered supports topped off by a genuine thatched roof. The two-story buildings front had two windows on the second floor and one large window on the side on the first floor. A small entryway protruded out, covering a well-constructed wooden front door, all of which were also covered by a thatched roof. A small shed was attached to one side of the building near a very well-built chimney. As far as English buildings were concerned, this was the cottage of our dreams. To make things even better than it looked, there was a stone marker on the path leading up to the door. It had the legend printed on it that said, 'Poachers Rest Cottage, built 1763.' We had always thought that our home back in Minnesota, which Ole's father had built in 1963, was old. Well, jump back in time some 200-plus years to our new place of dwelling.

Ole opened the heavy wood front door as its hinges made a groan of needing to be oiled. The large window on one side lets in enough light to see things. A very old-style push-button light control was needed to really light the place up. Of course, light it up was a bit of an understatement as the old electrical system with low-wattage light bulbs gave off about as much light as an early Edison lighting system.

The main part of the room still resembled the pub that this cottage had originally housed. A wood bar was still along one wall, and for now, a single dining room table and chairs were located where there had once been pub tables for the customers. A door behind the bar led us to the kitchen, which had been updated with a microwave and even an air-fryer.

On the opposite end of the cottage was a large fireplace. The walls were decorated with old family photos and a few sentimental knick-knacks, which we were sure had meaning to our forebearers, but they didn't have any memories for us. The fireplace room had been transformed into a sort of den with some bookcases, comfy chairs, and even a large flat-screen television. At least great-grandpa had a few modern conveniences.

As for the lighting, some new LED lights would make a heck of an improvement. Beneath the stairs was the 'wc' or 'loo' as we were learning to call the bathroom. It was probably the most modern room on the first floor. It was done in stone with a shower and large walk-in bathtub, which meant Lord Long was probably getting a bit feeble in his old age. A granite countertop held two sinks with a large mirror on the wall. A small high-efficiency furnace was tucked into one corner with a forced air system to heat the whole house. Other than the lighting, the rest of the house seemed to be very up-to-date. Maybe Lord Long didn't see well enough to care.

There were Viking ship plaques on the walls, and Viking figures were scattered about the room. Seemed somewhat strange if it were true that Ole's forebearers had fought the Vikings. It could be that it was Lord Long's way of marking a victory over his ancestor's enemies or honoring their dead. However, Ole was half Norwegian from his father's side, so he liked the décor a lot.

It had been a long day, and we were both 'dog' tired. Me even more so than Ole because I actually am a dog. We decided to stay inside for the evening and just relax. Ole heated up a can of Dinty Moore beef stew for our super, along with a bottle. Yes, you read that right, a real honest-to-goodness glass bottle of 7-up soda that was in the refrigerator.

We settled into a nice comfy chair in the theater room with its big screen television and were pleasantly surprised to see that we had internet access to a wide variety of programs and movies.

We picked out a movie we had never heard of, and it proved to be an excellent choice. It starred Morgan Freeman, who makes any movie he is in great, in our opinion. The movie was made in 2012 and was called 'The Magic of Belle Island.' If you haven't seen it, you should; both Ole and I highly recommend it. By the end of the movie, it was getting late, so we hit the sack for the night. Tomorrow we would start to explore our new surroundings.

CHAPTER 5

Looking out the window, we were greeted by a fog so thick we couldn't even see the mountain that was only a few feet away. We had, of course, heard about English fog in the many old movies we had watched; Hound of the Baskervilles immediately comes to mind. But this was more like a white sheet from a bed than actual fog. How does that old saying go? 'Fog so thick you can cut it with a knife.' Yes, sir, this was that kind of fog.

I went outside to do my morning duty, and it was so foggy I had trouble even locating a bush to relieve myself. Going back inside, I suggested to Ole that we wait until this blanket of fog dissipated before going to explore our surroundings.

It was early afternoon before the fog lifted. The sun was now shining, and tendrils of steam rose from the wet grass as the temperature rose into a nice comfortable range.

Making our way outside, we walked to the railway tracks and turned to face our new home. We had been in such a rush yesterday to get into our new adobe that we had not taken in the grander or the isolation of the Poachers Rest. No visible civilization was near us. Off in the distance, we could see the village of Hedgehoghaven. The cottage was nestled into a section of Longhall Mountain surrounded by trees and bushes. Off to the north, we could see the ruins of Longhall Castle and its keep. A bit farther north and barely visible from our vantage point was the mine, which was mentioned as part of our inheritance. What they mined, we had no idea, but supposedly the mine helped to pay some of the expenses. Making our way to the rear of the cottage, we could see it was only a few yards from the cottage's back door to the face of the mountain. Ole looked up and commented. "I sure hope there are no loose boulders up there, or we might be in for a rude awakening someday."

Once a brief exploration of our surroundings was over, we were anxious to go into the village of Hedgehoghaven and see just what kind of place it was.

There were no vehicles at the Poachers Rest, so driving into the village was not an option. So it seemed we had two options left open to us. One was that we had been told that we could call the Hedgehoghaven train station any time day or night, and they would dispatch a locomotive and passenger coach right to the door of our cottage, pick us up, and take us to the train station which was near the heart of the village. Our second option was just on the other side of the tracks from our cottage. A well-worn path that showed signs of tire tracks, so it seemed possible that our benefactor had at one time or another owned a vehicle and was able to use it to go back and forth to the village without the use of his private train. Of course, having a private train at our beck and call was awesome. It just didn't seem practical or cost-effective, seeing we were now the ones that had to worry about the financial well-being of Longhall County. It was also, to say the least, a bit pretentious.

With all things now considered, we decided to follow the path and walk into town. Ole being a bit crippled up from years of too much abuse to his body, grabbed his cane from the cottage, and off we went. This also gave us the opportunity to see if the path was wide enough and in reasonable condition to handle motorized transportation. One thing you should know is that both Ole and I are getting to that age where walking long distances is not at the top or even the middle of things that we like or are even capable of doing for any sustained period of time.

We soon learned that the visual distance of the village from our cottage seemed to be a lot closer than the walking distance. Although we did find that walking the path, it would sustain the use of a smaller size vehicle and certainly not one of the big American pick-up trucks or SUVs that are so prevalent back in the States.

By the time we reached the village, we were about pooped out. Ole's bad back was acting up, and I was panting like a dog in heat. Luckily for us, the path ended at the dual mainline railroad tracks, and once we had crossed them, it was just a short distance to a place called Chaps Pub, which meant a place to sit, beer to quench our thirst, and a chance to see some of the local colors. Plus, we had been informed by Mr. Fische, our solicitor, that this was the main hub of activity for the village.

It was still early in the day, so there were only a few people in the pub, and the looks we got did not seem very friendly or welcoming except for the bartender or, as the English referred to him the Publican. He gave us a welcome greeting. I suppose because he had met us on the train coming in and prompted by the fact that we were about to spend money in his establishment.

"Good day Sir and canine." He gave us a wink to let us know that he was pretending not to know us. "My names Casey the owner and operator of this fine establishment. I've not seen you in here before. If I may be so bold as to ask your names."

Ole: "My name is Ole and this little lady at my side is Tesse. Hopefully it is all right for her to be in here?"

Casey: "It's perfectly fine. Our town regulations say that all of Hedgehoghaven Village and any establishment within the confines of Longhall County are canine friendly. Tesse can go anywhere that you go in this county. Now, what can I get you two to drink?"

Ole: "I don't suppose you would have a nice cold SvenBrew on tap or if not maybe in a bottle?"

I hopped up on the stool next to Ole and waited in anticipation for a cold bowl of brew.

We heard a voice from one of the men at a corner table who muttered, "Damn, Yank." Casey threw a nasty glance at the man before he spoke. "Sorry, sir, I assume you're not from around here or anywhere in the United Kingdom. The custom here is room-temperature beer by the pint. I've never heard of a beer called SvenBrew. I have some local beer brewed right here from hops grown in this very county. Would you like to try it? The first one is on the house."

Ole: "Your friend back in the corner is right. I am a yank from America. I'll have a pint of your local brew with two green olives in it and Tesse will have a bowl of the same without olives, she's never really acquired a taste for them."

Casey: "I've got a supply of dog treats here, I can toss one in her beer if you think she would like it?"

I quickly communicated to Ole that a dog treat in my beer was a great idea. I can't believe I never thought of it before.

As we partook in our liquid refreshments, Casey supplied us with a bowl of pretzels. A wink of his eye alerted us to listen closely as he whispered. "I'm going to pretend I don't know who you are. You can make that announcement when you feel it's appropriate. No need to roust the locals just yet."

Casey: "From the colonies you say. What brings you here? We're sort of off the beaten path for most folks. Not really a tourist destination if you know what I mean. You here for the day or staying for a while. Nice hotel just around the corner if you need overnight accommodations."

We weren't really sure just how much information we should give at the moment. The gentlemen in the corner did not seem too happy to see a 'yank' in their midst. Casey was putting on a good show, so we figured to just play along until the time was right.

Ole: "We plan on staying in the area for a while. Thank you for the suggestion of the hotel, we may have to think about it but for now we'll make do staying at a place a friend suggested to us."

The man in the corner spoke up again. "What friend? What place? I know everyone in the village and every place that's available. I have not heard from anyone of any visitors coming here."

Casey: "That's enough from you Whiskey Steve. You best mind your own business. This gentlemen and his dog are customers of mine and they don't have to answer any questions if they don't want to. Any more lip from you and I'll cut you off the drink for a week."

Whiskey Steve: "Don't get your panties in a bunch Casey. I was just asking is all."

Ole and I decided it was probably best that we leave for the time being. We finished our beers, and Ole quietly, so as not to be overheard by the other patrons of the pub, asked Casey if there was somewhere in the village where we might be able to purchase a vehicle.

Casey whispered back that we should check out Tony's Cycle & Auto on the southwest end of the village. He mentioned it was next to the fire station as an easy landmark for us to find the place.

Leaving the pub under the watchful unfriendly eyes of the two men at the table, we headed west. We passed an imposing old two-story abandoned building. Ole stopped for a moment and looked over the structure with its grey stone exterior, columned flanked front door, and turret-style attachment on the corner.

Ole: "Tesse, I think we should look into taking this place over. I have a great idea for it. A building with this much personality should not be sitting empty."

We rounded the corner, and down at the far end of the block was Tony's place. The hose drying tower of the fire station was clearly visible but not really needed as a landmark for Tony's was easily visible from our vantage point.

We walked along the block and looked over the businesses as we passed them to start familiarizing ourselves with the layout of the village. The first building was Lovett's Lamb & Meats Butcher Shop. Next was a fish and chips restaurant called 'In Cod We Trust,' what a great name. Then came the Post Office, the Kings Head Hotel, Henry's Hardware & General Store, the Police Station, and lastly, at the end of the block was the Pickwick Book store. I had to steer Ole clear of the bookstore until a later time as we were on a mission to find transportation and not browse through what, in Ole's case, would be hundreds of books.

To the west of us, across the street, was the main Hedgehoghaven Train Station, which looked to be a busy place. Just west of the Station was a building in the shape of a bulldog and appropriately named the Bulldog Café. Near the café was a parking lot set off with a large steam engine called the Winston Churchill. Down from the parking lot and across the two mainline railway tracks was another train station that served the outer line railway tracks, while the main and busier of the two stations serviced the inner mainline, which was more heavily used from the look of things.

Crossing the street to Tony's, we got a good look at the fire station. A fire truck and ambulance sitting outside were being cleaned and polished by two firemen. Next to the fire station was a graveyard surrounded by a stone wall and nestled next to what we would later learn was St. Catherine's Church.

Tony's place was typical of a garage repair shop like Ole was used to back when he was a kid in Minnesota. A few old cars scattered about, and a junker car being salvaged for parts sat alongside the building. Two old gas pumps on our front and a mixture of oil and tire displays, along with an assorted jumble of miscellaneous motorcycle and car parts, were scattered about. A 1972 green MG car was parked in the garage with its hood 'or is that bonnet' up, and a man was bent over the fender tinkering with the engine. A Triumph motorcycle with a sidecar was at the gas pump and was just getting ready to pull away.

The 'L' shaped building was made of brick, with a single-stall garage taking up the majority of space. A small office jutted out of the west end of the building. Above the garage was a large sign 'Tony's Cycle & Auto."

We opened the door to the office and looked inside. Normal clutter and a smell of gas and oil assaulted our nostrils, but no one was in sight. We heard a voice coming from the garage asking us if we wanted something. We headed in the direction of the voice. We approached the MG, and a head popped up from under the bonnet. A slightly balding man in his forties looked us over.

"Hello, I'm Tony. I own this place. What can I help you with?"

Ole: "My name's Ole and this is my canine partner Tesse. Casey from Chaps Pub told us that you might be able to help us out. We just moved here and are in need of some transportation. I'd prefer a motorcycle with a sidecar if you happen to have one or know of one for sale."

Tony: "It just so happens that I purchased one from a chap over in Norway. The puffer ship Carolsea just brought it over a few days ago. It's got a rather unusual paint job so it's a bit unique. I plan on repainting it before I put it up for sale. You can take a peek at it and tell me if ou're interested. On second thought it's not actually a motorcycle it's a 2003 Honda 600cc Silverwing scooter with a sidecar. Plenty of power. It might just fit the bill for you."

Tony led us to the back corner of the garage and pulled a tarp off a bright yellow checker-stripped scooter with a sidecar with what was reminiscent of what we remembered seeing on a Yellow Cab back in the United States. The rear had a picture of a Viking Longship and the words Norwegian Taxi. Ole, being of partial Norwegian descent, fell instantly in love with it. I just hoped he didn't give away his immediate desire to own it and was going to haggle over the price.

Ole held his excitement in check. "How much you want for it just the way it is. Of course I expect it to be in good running condition."

Tony: "I already went through it so it's ready to ride. If I don't have to repaint it. 3,670 pounds."

Ole: "Not to be rude, but that seems a bit high. After all, it is 2003, and you won't have to repaint it. I'll give you 2,250 pounds.

Tony: "2,580 and you've got a deal."

So for about $3,500 dollars American in the coin of our thinking, we now owned a scooter with a sidecar. Ole paid Tony, and he handed Ole the keys. We pushed the scooter outside, and I hopped into the sidecar. As far as I was concerned, I was going to love my sidecar; plenty of room for me, and I could feel the wind in my fur and take in the open breezes with all their associated aromas.

As we drove out of the gas station, a blast of a horn from an oncoming vehicle quickly reminded us being in England, we were on the wrong side of the road. Something we had better get used to very quickly.

We headed east past a large building called Williams Yard Repairs and Restorations. A group of men in uniforms that we would later learn was the county Home Guards were conducting military maneuvers. Although nationally, the Home Guard had been disbanded in 1945 after World War Two; it seems that Longhall County kept its unit intact, just in case. Better safe than sorry. The Williams building had an arched opening large enough to accommodate most vehicles and allowed access to a street that served the rear entrances to most of the downtown businesses. A quick glance showed that there was one business located within this semi-enclosed area. It was called Kilroy's Slot Shop and had a large Kilroy figure peaking over the peak of the roof.

As we turned the corner at St. Catherine's Church, we saw the Village clock tower on the corner of the street, which held the east side of the village's main street businesses.

The first building was Ye Olde Tea Shoppe. Then Dingmann's Clothing Store and Mortuary were a rather strange combination, but at least there were separate entrances for the two businesses which occupied the same building. The next building was empty, with a for rent sign plastered on its front. Then came Dr. John's Dentist, Doctor, Medicine with a large row of teeth along the bottom edge of the roof and a large tooth jutting out from the front of the building, a small arched opening on the far end of the building allowed access to the center court that made up the rear of the town business district and of course was also accessible from the Williams building. Olson's Slot Shoppe was next, and then an empty building that we quickly decided we would occupy with our old business from Minnesota, The Odditorium gift shop. Next up was Natural Healing Massage, Tracey's Fruit & Vegetables, Archie's Bakery, Hedgehoghaven Movie Theater, and at the very corner Kelley's Centimental Coin-ops Arcade.

On the opposite side of the street was Rocky's Tavern, Olive's Restaurant, a small gas station, and the village park, which was surrounded by a Cotswold stone wall.

As a footnote, we noticed Carol's Stable off from the rear and across the tracks from the church and a bustling wharf behind Tony's place. We debated stopping at the little restaurant across from the main street, but instead, we were too anxious to see if our new mode of transportation would handle the planked railroad track crossing and the dirt road that led back to the Poachers Rest.

We eased the Norwegian Taxi over the railroad crossing and then made our way down the narrow pathway to our cottage. Some of the areas were a bit rutted and had some nasty potholes, but by taking our time and maneuvering around the worst areas, we got back to our starting point with no major problems. However, we decided on our next trip to the village; we would take a pail of dirt with us and start filling in and smoothing out some of the potholes and tamping them down to smooth out our future rides.

We spent the rest of the day exploring our new home and the immediate property around it. Tomorrow we would head back to the village and introduce ourselves to some of the locals.

CHAPTER 6

Come morning, we were up early and ready to head to the village and start getting to know some of the people. However, we were once again greeted by fog that was rolling onto the land from the sea. The smell of the sea and damp foliage filled our nostrils. It was not unpleasant, but it was not the same aroma that the water and fog of the Mississippi River back home gave off. Under the circumstances and with limited visibility, we decided to postpone our trip for the time being.

It was noon before the fog lifted. Ole found a bucket and shovel so we could scavenge some dirt from around our place. With the bucket filled and a shovel ready, we put them on the floor in the sidecar, and with me taking up the sidecar seat, off we went.

We stopped at the first good-sized hole on our little road to the village, and it quickly ate up our bucket full of dirt. Ole tamped the fresh earth into the hole, and then we proceeded on to the village. There was no doubt it would take many trips to repair our road. With our commitment to live in England, we would have lots of time to putz around fixing up our little pathway to civilization, if that is what the village could be considered.

We crossed the railroad tracks and parked our Norwegian Taxi along the stone wall near the park. We walked past Kelley's Arcade, Chaps Pub and the empty building on the corner. Rounding the corner past Lovett's Lambs & Meat, we entered In 'Cod We Trust.' An A-frame sandwich-style sign near the door was held by a smiling fish announcing the day's special. Fish & Chips. We would eventually learn the 'days' special never changed. It was always 'Fish & Chips.'

Inside we were greeted by a jovial fellow about 5' 7" tall, heavy set, wavy dark hair and rosy red cheeks.

"Top of the afternoon, Sir and canine. My name's Winton, owner, cook and bottle washer of this fine dining establishment. I'd offer you a menu but there is none. You get today's special. In fact, it's the same special every day. Fish & chips. If your canine companion is eating, she pays the same price as you."

I hopped up on a chair next to Ole at one of the small round tables in the place and mentioned to him that the sign-out front was very accurate. There were only two items on the menu fish & chips. Of course, there were drinks available. I ordered my meal with a bowl of water, and Ole had a bottle of Squirt soda.

Winton: "Haven't seen you two before. Visitor's I suppose. Not much here to see. Or, maybe you come off one of the boats in the harbor? If so, you must be new crew members as I know most of the boat men and crews here abouts."

Ole: "Actually, we are moving here from the States."

Winton: "I figured you were a yank from your accent. Why the hell would you move here? Hedgehoghaven ain't known for a place to be making a new start in life or retiring if that's what you have a mind for. Either someone sold you a fake bill of goods, or you're daft. Also, ain't no cottages to buy or rent unless you plan on living at the King's Head Hotel. You would need mighty deep pockets to take up permanent residence at the hotel."

Ole: "It's possible we were sold a bill of goods, or more likely, we are daft as you say. We've got a permanent home here. We've taken up residence at the Poachers Rest."

Winton: "Daft as a loony bird you is! That place isn't for sale or rent. That place belongs to the late Sir Aaron Long. Finer fellow you never did meet, but he's now dead and buried in the graveyard at St. Catherine's. Anyone catches you living at the Poachers Rest, and the Bobbies will toss you in the clink quicker than you can blink an eye. That goes for your wee little dog too."

Ole: "I don't think we have to worry about that. I just inherited the Poachers Rest and all of Longhall County, including the village of Hedgehoghaven and the railroad, from my great-grandfather Lord Aaron Long. My name is Ole, and this is my canine companion Tesse."

Winton: "Well I'll be bloody flabbergasted. You're the new owner of Longhall County! Just imagine a 'yank' having his very own little English Dynasty. You told anyone else about this?"

Ole: "Not yet. Although the two fellows who brought us here by train know. They've been sworn to secrecy."

Winton: "May I be so bold as to ask their names, Lord Ole."

Ole: "You may, but only if you drop the 'Lord' and just call me Ole. It was Casey and Captain Pierce."

Winton: "Casey owns Chaps Pub, and he must be drinkin' himself silly trying to keep the news to himself. Captain Pierce, he'll act like he's the Duke of the realm now and claim you're his best friend. You and Tesse are going to be big news around here. Just wait and see,"

Ole: "We really just want to try and fit in and not cause a fuss. I thought maybe we would let a few folks know, like you, and maybe stop over to Chaps Pub and sort of ease who we are in a non-formal way to a few of the regulars there. I'm sure word will spread on its own."

Winton: "Bloody brilliant idea. You two finish up with your meal; it's on the house. Nothing is too good for the Lord of the Realm. I'm going to lock the place up for the day, and the three of us can go over to Chaps. I'm buying the beers."

Ole: "You don't need to do that. I don't want you to close your shop and lose money. Certainly, you don't need to buy drinks for us or anyone else."

Winton: "Hell, I don't. I wouldn't miss this for all the cod in the world. I'm tired of working for the day anyways. We'll all go get falling drunk and have a merry ol' time. Once word spreads, which won't take long, the pub will be bursting at the seams."

By the time we had finished eating, Winton had taken off his apron and put on a suit coat and a tie. He was standing by the door key in the lock, waiting for us to head out so he could lock the place up.

Winton led the way, and as we rounded the corner towards the pub, we noticed a large crowd had gathered outside on the grass in front of the pub. Two boxers were standing almost toe-to-toe. One was wearing white boxer trunks, and the other had red-white-blue boxer trunks. Both wore red boxing gloves.

We could hear the boxer in the white trunks taunting the other boxer. "You're just a movie star boxer wanna-be." With threats and promises of putting him down for the count in three-rounds. The boxer in red-white-blue trunks stoically stood there taking the threats and with a slow drawled answer of "Maybe so, maybe not."

Ole looked at Winton and said. "I know it's not possible, but one of them is deceased, and the other is way too old to actually be boxing, but I'd swear those two boxers are dead ringers for Muhammad Ali and Sylvester Stallone as Rocky Balboa."

Winton: "Something you will soon learn when you live in Longhall County is that time is flexible. This is where legends live, and reality dies. Anything is possible here. The upcoming boxing match is an exhibition match with all proceeds going to the save the Hedgehog fund."

I told Ole to ask about my seeing Paddington Bear at the train station.

Ole: "I know this may sound silly, but is it possible that Paddington Bear could have been at the train station when we arrived here? Or was it just a human dressed up in a costume to look like Paddington Bear?"

Winton: "Oh yes, Paddington, no human in a custom, my friend. Paddington loves to travel by train, and Hedgehoghaven is one of his favorite places to visit. Besides living legends, fantasy tends to merge with reality here in Longhall County."

I had to wonder, as did Ole, just what kind of place we had inherited. Dead and fading legends hanging around the Village, imaginary animals like Paddington Bear come to life. Just what else we would discover as time went on was anyone's guess.

As Winton led the way through the crowd that was watching the two boxers, Ole bumped into a man with a brown fedora hat, brown leather jacket and a whip in one hand. Ole quickly excused himself and then stared at the man as he said. "You're Harrison Ford."

The man looked at Ole straight-faced and answered. "I am not Harrison Ford. I'm Indiana Jones. But you can call me Indy if you like."

Things just seemed to be getting weirder all the time.

We entered Chaps Pub, and although the biggest crowd was outside, there were still a fair amount of people in the pub drinking and talking about the upcoming exhibition match. A fellow named Kilroy was busy taking bets on the outcome of the match. Seems he owned Kilroy's Slot Machine shop which was located in the courtyard in the center of the village. Being a dealer in slot machines, it was only natural that he was also the local 'bookie' for the village. So far, it seems that the odds of the boxing match were slightly in favor of Muhammad Ali at this time.

Winton made his way through the crowd and laid claim to an open table for us. He went to the bar and soon returned with two pints and a bowl of beer. He took a long swig of his beer and then stood up on his chair with his pint of beer in hand. He hollered out for everyone to be quiet and pay attention. Actually, he had to repeat his request three times before the place finally quieted down and looked at him.

Winton: "I have an announcement to make, and best all of you pay attention. It seems our friend and benefactor Lord Aaron Long, who we all know passed from this earthly realm a while back, has left his estate, which of course, includes all of Longhall County and our little village of Hedgehoghaven to his great-grandson. His only heir. So I am going to buy one and only one round of beer for the house." Which, of course, brought out a rousing cheer from all in attendance.

Winton: "Quiet! No drinks served until I finish. So, without further ado I would like to present to all of you Lord Ole and his faithful companion Tesse."

Winton lifted his pint of beer in the air and asked everyone to join him with three cheers for Lord Ole and Tesse. "Now to the bar for your free beer!"

Ole and I were rather embarrassed by this rousing introduction and welcome for the pubs patrons. Ole did his best to accept the congratulations as he stood up and weakly waved to the crowd.

Speech, speech came a roar from those in attendance. Many, of course, had been imbibing in spirits in anticipation of the soon-to-be-held boxing match.

Winton got down from his chair and forcibly pushed and cajoled Ole to stand on his chair and give a speech.

Reluctantly Ole got up on the chair. "Thank you all for the warm welcome." We could hear distinct murmurs going through the crowd, with the word 'yank' being very prevalent. "I'm form the United States, as if my accent has not yet given me away. All this title stuff, like being a 'Lord' is a bit foreign to me, and so I would prefer to just be addressed as Ole. I have heard my great-grandfather was well-liked by most of the village and that he was fair and easy to work with or for, as the case may be. I will do my best to follow his example. I have a lot to learn, and I hope all of you will help me to learn your ways and to fit in as best as Tesse and I can. We have moved into the Poachers Rest, which I was told was my great-grandfather's home. With that being said, the next round of beer is on me."

Ole got a rousing cheer, probably not for his speech but for buying a round of beer.

One thing was certain. Although most of Longhall County was here for the boxing match, there was little doubt that by the end of the day, everyone would know about Lord Ole and me.

Lots of folks stopped by our table to say hello and introduce themselves. Maybe they were just being friendly, or maybe they had ulterior motives and would come calling later for special favors. Ole was always one to look for the best in people, me, being a canine, was a bit more skeptical. My senses tended to be able to pick out the sincere folks from the ones who were just putting on an act. If you want to judge a person's motives, it's always best to ask a dog for their opinion.

The boxing match was about to start, and the pub emptied out faster than stink from a skunk. We were quickly overshadowed by the sporting event, so we joined the crowd and went outside to watch the match. It was to be a five-round exhibition match, and it was quite a sight to see. Both men were boxing as if in their prime. By the end of the fifth round, it was hard to say what the judge's decision would be. Guess what, I'm not going to tell you.

Ole and I aren't crazy about big crowds and lots of activities, so as soon as the match was over, we slipped away. Boarding the Norwegian Taxi, we high-tailed it back to the Poachers Rest. We would go back to the village tomorrow after things had settled down and were a bit quieter and more laid back then they were today.

CHAPTER 7

The next morning we took off early for the village. It would be a nice peaceful time to check out the area businesses at our leisure. We filled our bucket with dirt and made a few stops along the way filling in more holes and slowly making our little roadway more comfortable.

Wandering around the village, which was laid out in a square with an open courtyard in the center we soon discovered Pickwick Books. The young lady in charge was named Erica; she had dark hair and a bit of a sassy attitude. She often peeked out the door to make sure the boy outside was hawking the village's weekly newspaper and not letting any potential customers sneak by him.

Ole is an avid reader, and since we had to bypass this place when we were on our mission to buy some transportation, we now had time for him to browse to his heart's content. Erica pointed out the large selection of books, new and used, plus a wide variety of magazines. She made a point to let Ole know that the items in her store were for sale and not just for browsing. I decided to sit outside and enjoy the so-far rare morning of sunshine in this land of fog.

Forty-five minutes later, Ole finally emerged from the book store with a bag in his hand. "What did you buy?" I asked.

Ole: "They actually had a few books from the world's greatest unknown author 'Hells Lefse.' I snagged a rare first edition of 'Dogpire.' I can read it to you tonight.

On the other side of the road was a new-looking building done in blue and white with a skylight window on the roof. It was called 'Heck of a Deal' CFMoto ATV and side-by-side vehicles. It was run by a fellow named Tony Heck. He told us that everyone just called him 'Heck' so as not to cause any confusion with the other 'Tony' of the repair shop.

Heck showed us the CFMoto side-by-sides and their ATV line and mentioned that they would soon be adding motorcycles to the line-up. We had to admit they had some impressive machines with lots of features and a very reasonable price point.

However, there was a sad point to Heck's story. It seems he had only built and opened his shop a few months ago. He had hastily put up a pre-fabricated building under cover of darkness in one night without the approval of the village council. The village voted that Heck's building did not meet the requirements of the village charter, which stated that any structures had to follow certain guidelines and fit in with the old-world charm and architecture of the rest of the village. Looking over Heck's building, it was rather out of place with its modern pre-fab look.

This dilemma left Heck with two choices. He could fight the village council, which of course, was a forgone losing proposition. Or, he could tear down his new building and build again under the village guidelines.

However, he opted for a third option. CFMoto hired him to be a district representative for their company so they could expand into more markets. He accepted their offer and then arranged for Tony's repair shop to take over his existing franchise. Thus Tony would buy the remaining inventory from Heck, who could then set up his first new dealer as district manager. Problem solved.

Of course, his existing new building would still have to be removed. Heck located a pub in a neighboring village that was being forced out by expansion. Just the opposite of what was happening here. Hedgehoghaven village was not in favor of expansion as it was happy just the way it was. Heck's soon-to-be empty lot was still open for business according to the village council. Heck made a deal that he would absorb half the cost of removing his building. The pub that was to move in would absorb the other half of the cost and move onto the spot of Heck's now-defunct business as Heck put it. "Better to lose half my investment instead of all of it."

A week later, the Hedgehoghaven Railway stopped near the now-empty lot of Tony Heck's now-removed building. The train had a center depressed eight wheeled flat cars with the small Rocky's Tavern building on it. Sheets of steel and steel girders surrounded the tavern to keep it in one piece. A railway crane was brought in to lift the brick structure form the flat car to skids on the ground.

It was only a short distance from the tracks to the block basement that had been dug for the Tavern's foundation. Once the Tavern was in place, it would be just a few days for the electricity and water to be hooked up. Rocky's didn't look like it would be much competition for Casey's Chaps Pub, but at least it would give everyone a choice of drinking establishments.

We spent the next week puttering around the Poachers Rest and doing our best to make it our own. Most of the pictures on the wall of our forbearers luckily had names and dates on brass plaques below them. This allowed us to look up their histories on the computer. Like any family, there were a few black sheep in the flock.

There were four bedrooms upstairs from when the cottage was a pub and boarding house. We chose the largest for ourselves. It looks to have been the master bedroom with a fireplace, a large four-poster bed, and still contained many of great–grandfather's things, which we packed into some old trunks with care for the storage. Two of the other bedrooms were just that, bedrooms with beds. The fourth bedroom was full of old boxes of junk that people tend to accumulate, thinking someday they may have a use for it. A 'loo' was also on this floor with just a shower, toilet and small sink.

Ole had a plan for the 'junk' room. Possibly he could build a model railroad there and add in a few slot machines, which were another of his passions.

For our next trip to the village, Ole and I made a list of light bulbs that needed to be replaced with LEDs to brighten the place up. Slowly but surely, we would make the Poachers Rest our 'home.'

We took the Norwegian Taxi over the railroad tracks and around the stone wall that limited access to the village from our direction and made our way to Henry's Hardware store. Henry was a tall, lanky fellow with short red hair and a complexion so fair it would make a vampire blush with envy. He was very helpful in showing us lighting options and suggesting the best ones for our use. His son, Oscar, with curly blonde hair and a complexion like his father's, was quick to volunteer to load our purchases into our sidecar.

Our next stop was to check out Rocky's Tavern. It was now settled onto the lot previously occupied by 'Heck of a Deal CFMoto.' The brick building was very old and well-weathered. We had to marvel that it had actually made it to its new location in one piece. It actually looked as if it had been in its present location for years. Garbage cans along one of the outside walls next to the cellar doors and some empty wood crates along with a few scattered empty beer bottles added to its charm. A man passed out against one of the garbage cans with a half-empty bottle of spirits in his hand was the crowning touch of a well-established drinking establishment. It was rather amusing to think that a place that had just settled in could look so at home.

We decided to give some support to this new business in the village, so we went inside. The inside was not much different than the outside for age. The owner greeted us with a friendly, "Hello, chaps. I'm Rocky. What can I get you?"

Rocky was reminiscent of a leftover biker from the 1960s rocker culture of Britain. Greased back pompadour hairdo, white t-shirt with a pack of cigarettes rolled up in the sleeve, grease-stained blue jeans with rolled up cuffs with a thick black leather belt and motorcycle chain belt buckle, black leather motorcycle boots and a black leather jacket hung on a hook behind the bar to complete his ensemble. We assumed the Triumph motorcycle in the parking lot was his.

Ole sat on one of the well-worn barstools, and I jumped up on the one next to him. Looking around the place, it was easy to see the building had been moved with all its original furnishings.

The walls were covered with framed photos of past Kings and Queens with brass plates below them. Queen Victoria 1832-1901, King Edward VII 1901-1910, King George V 1910-1936, King Edward VIII 1936, King George VI 1936-1952, and Queen Elizabeth II 1952-2022 and King Charles 2022-present.

Posters and photos from both World Wars were scattered about along with pictures of Winston Churchill. Then there were the real photographs of airplanes, tanks, soldiers and even the horrors of the blitz. It was like we were about to have a drink in a time machine.

For amusement, along one wall was a well-worn dart board and a shelf that held a very well-used Allwin Defiant slot machine. This was a conversion game made during World War two when materials were scarce, and national pride in supporting the war effort was popular.

Ole: "I don't suppose you have a nice cold SvenBrew beer on tap?"

Rocky: "Never heard of it, mate. You must be a Yank; I can tell by your accent and the fact that you would actually prefer your beer to be 'cold.'

I've got Carling, Fosters, Carlsberg, Coors Lite, Tennets, Heineken, Amstel or Kronenbourg. Just between you and me, I just got a couple of cases of 'Two Women' beer. It's a nice refreshing lager that Captain Pierce offered me at a decent price. Seems he smuggled some in from Wisconsin, located in the colonies. Just keep that information, hush, mate. We wouldn't want the good Captain to get in trouble. He got it for me as a favor for the grand opening of my new location. You're one of my first customers since I set up shop here, so I thought I'd give you a chance to taste something form the colonies. Maybe cure any home sickness you may have."

Ole: "I've actually had Two Women beer before. For me and Tesse's taste, it's one of t best beers every. We'll have that."

Rocky: "It's not cheap. Four times as much as the local stuff, but worth it. You sure you want it?"

Ole: "We do."

Considering Ole had two bottles and I had one bottle in a bowl, we spent a few 'pounds' at Rocky's Tavern before we left. We figured Rocky would do all right as he was catering to the not so affluent if they didn't want Two Women beer. With the large number of motorcycles we had seen on the streets of the village, we were pretty sure this might turn into their place of choice for drinks and camaraderie.

We left Rocky's and went next door to a well-kept white wooden building with lots of colorful signs adorning the front. It was called Olive's Café. It was, of course, owned and run by a nice lady named Olive. We had a delicious hamburger, and fries topped off by her very own homemade ice cream for desert.

With full bellies, we were now ready to return to the Poachers Rest and start replacing the old incandescent lights with new up-to-date LEDs. Some of the old lights had covers and decorative shades and holders that had become a bid corroded and stiff from not having been removed for years. Occasional squirts of loosening oil and lots of muscle, and a few choice words from Ole finally prevailed. By early evening the cottage lighting was updated.

We were so excited that we turned on every light in the cottage, and then we went outside to admire our handiwork as anyone who passed by would see it. The place looked modern and bright through the windows, and even if no one else was around to impress, we were ecstatic at what we had accomplished. This all has to be taken into account, as Ole and I are not what you would call very handy when it comes to fixing things.

CHAPTER 8

We hung around the cottage for most of the day. At 6 pm, we decided to head to Chaps Pub for a sandwich and a beer.

Entering Chaps, we were greeted by Casey, who was behind the bar. Archie, the owner of the Pastry Shop, and Doug, owner of Dingmann's Clothier and Mortuary. Lates, the postman, John the dentist and Captain Pierce invited us to join them at their table.

We graciously accepted their offer. Casey brought over beers and snacks for everyone except Lates, who had his regular order of Nehi grape soda with a slice of raisin pie. After introductions had been made, the small talk started.

Lates: "So you're the new Lord of the Realm. If you ever need any help finding any place around here, just let me know. I deliver mail to everyone in the county no matter how close or far away they are."

Archie took a few chips from the bowl and then removed his false teeth, and dropped them into his beer.

John: "Do you have to do that?"

Archie: "Yes. You know I can't eat with the darn things in my mouth. Too uncomfortable."

John: "If you'd make an appointment at my office I could fix you with some dentures that would fit and be comfortable for you."

Archie: "You just want my money. The dentist that made these darn things said the same thing."

John: "At least buy a plastic case to put them in. Having them smiling at all of us in the bottom of your beer glass is sort of discomforting."

Doug: "It's not that bad. I've seen worse trying to adjust them in some cadaver's mouth so they'll look good in their casket at the funeral. Sometimes I have to take them out because it just isn't working out, leaving them in. In fact, I've got a whole bucket full of them back at my shop. Archie, you should stop by and try some on; maybe find a set that would be comfortable for you."

Archie: "I might just do that. How much do you want for them?"

Doug: "You find a set you like, and there yours for a pint of beer."

Pierce: "That's enough about Archie's teeth. Doug, you have been keeping my casket polished up for me?"

Doug: "Yes."

Archie: "Ole, I bet you never seen the likes of ol' Piercy there. He likes to go over to the mortuary and lie in his casket to see if it fits him all right."

Pierce: "Nothing wrong with that. If I have to spend the rest of eternity in it, I want to know I'll be comfortable."

Lates: "I think it's a bit morbid."

Archie: "Pierce has a point. It's not such a bad idea."

John: "You would think it was a good idea. You keep your teeth in the bottom of your beer glass."

Archie: "Show's what you know. When I finish my beer, I put my teeth back in my mouth, and I can savor the taste of my beer for hours afterwards."

Doug: "Lord Ole, what do you think about trying on a casket for size?"

Ole: "First off, I'm not comfortable with being called Lord. Ole will do just fine. As for trying on a casket for size, I think personally I would pass on that idea."

Pierce: "Talking about royalty."

John: "Who was talking about royalty?"

Pierce: "Ole was. He mentioned he preferred that we not call him 'Lord." That's sort of like royalty."

Lates: "Whatever. I know where this is leading."

Doug: "Me too. We better get more beer."

Pierce: "Ole, you're new here, so I'll tell you about my brush with royalty. It was a few years back. Queen Elizabeth was having a party, and she needed someone to entertain her guests, so she called me. She said Piercy, would you mind coming to the party and playing the piano and singing a few songs for my guests. She always called me Piercy, and I called her Queenie or sometimes Lizzy.

I said Lizzy, I'd be more than happy to entertain at your party. I arrived at the Royal Ballroom in my tuxedo and tails, along with a majestic top hat that I had made special just for the occasion.

I regaled her guests with my piano playing. Many of them thought my prowess on the keyboard made Liberace look like an amateur. Then I sang my world-famous rendition of the song 'Please release me let me go.'

Before I could even finish the song, some of those fancy ladies started tossing their room keys my way. Then a few panties with their names stitched into them landed around me so I would know whose they were with the hope that I may come and visit them in their boudoir. I'll tell you it was getting difficult to keep playing the piano as panties fell on the keyboard and got in my way. Finally, a bra was tossed my way and hooked itself on my ear. Lizzy just smiled at me, gave me a wink of her eye and suggested that I should probably end my performance before all the female guests would soon be completely naked."

Lates, John and Doug just shook their heads. They had heard this story one too many times.

Pierce: "They all think I just made it up, but it's true as the day is long."

Ole trying to be a sport, said. "Well, it can't be any stranger then Mohammed Ali and Rocky Balboa having an exhibition match here. Or my seeing Indiana Jones and Tesse seeing Paddington Bear."

Lates: "Those things are all real. You know the moto of Longhall County is Legends live, reality dies."

Ole and I were a bit dumbfounded by what these folks actually seemed to believe was true. Or was it that they were just putting us on with a cruel sense of humor. Mohammed Ali, Rocky Balboa, Indiana Jones and Paddington Bear might just have been actors dressed up to look like those people. If it was a joke, it was pretty elaborate. It seemed like now was a good time to change the subject.

Ole: "I'm a bit curious about how the village got its name?"

Lates: "That's pretty easy. Generations ago, some say, during the time of the Norse raiders, the Lord of Longhall County came to be. Lord Long, I made peace with the Vikings as the trading business became more profitable than the raiding of villages. That peace is what got him the county that is named after his family.

 Lord Long I had always had a soft spot for the wee creatures, and with more human encroachment on the hedgehog's natural environment, they were being forced from their natural habitat. Knowing that their main diet was eating insects and they were good for people's gardens and crops, he declared them a protected species. Plus, the little buggers are sort of cute."

When it was time for another round of beers, Ole made a big mistake. He asked Casey if he happened to have any 'Two Women' beer.

Casey: "You too? You're the second one to ask for it today. The first customer wouldn't tell me why. So how about you? What's this new found fascination with Two Women beer? I've never heard of it. Where did you try it?"

Ole could see where this was leading, and he didn't want to go there. He didn't want to get Rocky or Captain Pierce in trouble as Rocky told him how it had been smuggled in. As the better part of valor, Ole decided to tell a partial truth without elaborating. "I used to pick some up when I would travel through Wisconsin back in the States. It was always one of my favorites, along with SvenBrew. I know you don't carry SvenBrew, so I took a long shot and thought I would ask about Two Women."

Captain Pierce nervously rolled his glass around in his hands and looked away to make sure not to make eye contact with Casey. Ole did the same after his answer, being a bit ashamed and worried he might let the cat out of the bag and get Rocky and Captain Pierce in trouble.

Casey could see he was not about to get any answers to his question, so he asked if any of us wanted to order food. Everyone did, and Ole and I decided to split a Reuben sandwich and some onion rings.

More small talk followed until Casey came with our food. His wife Tracey had closed up her shop 'Tracey's Fruits & Vegetables for the day, as had his daughter, who closed up Tessa's Ye Old Tea Shoppe. They showed up at the pub to help out. This allowed Casey to join our group for a bit of comradery.

Ole: "Tesse and I are not only a bit new to the village but also to England. We love history and would really like to learn more about Longhall County and the village. One thing that interests us is the ruins of Longhall Castle, located on the mountain behind the Poachers Rest. There seem to be two sets of ruins there. Are they both from the original castle? They don't seem to be connected as one is on a different level than the other one."

Casey: "Best as anyone knows, the castle was built in the mid to late 1600s. It was situated on the mountain to allow a view of the sea so that an eye could be kept for possible Norse invaders. By the time the castle was actually completed, the threat from the Viking raiders had pretty much subsided. Peace between the Vikings and Longhall County had been established. It was about this time that Hedgehoghaven Village began to be established as a trading post.

The Castle was still considered a great deterrent to keep any other raiders from land or from the sea. The castle itself is located on the highest point of Longhall Mountain. The lower level structure with its tower is the castle keep. It was well fortified and was the first line of defense if the main castle should ever come under attack.

Lord Long I, his family and many descendants lived in the castle for hundreds of years. The castle was cold and damp and not the most comfortable of places to live. The thick stone walls tended to let moisture seep in from the damp fog and frequent rain that so often enveloped the mountain. Eventually, the mortar started to disintegrate as the years went by, and the castle began to crumble. It is said in its glory days; the castle was staffed by at least fifty servants. With the castle deteriorating and the cost to repair it combined with a shrinking of the Long family, it was no longer feasible to keep it up or to live there. Eventually, as the staff shrank along with the size of the Long family, it was decided that the castle and the keep be abandoned. Lord Long and his wife moved into the Poachers Rest. They had children, but none of them were interested in trying to keep up the castle or all of the lands associated with Longhall County. The children moved away and disappeared from their parents and any association with Longhall County. Now the ruins of the castle and the keep are all that is left of a once proud heritage."

Ole: "Does anyone ever give tours of the ruins? I would think it would be a great thing to do for tourists and school kids from our village and neighboring villages."

Doug: "Yes, it was a great idea. Until that movie company came here back in the 1940s."

Ole: "They made a movie here and at the castle? That's great, what a tourist draw."

Doug. "It didn't turn out so well."

Ole: "What happened?"

Pierce: "Someone thought like you. They figured to bring all the classic movie monsters together in one film. So Frankenstein's Monster and his bride, Dracula, Wolfman, the Mummy, and even a Gill-man from the Black Lagoon were all to be included in one great big monster extravaganza."

Archie: "Within days of filming, things started to go terribly wrong. The actors said they started to see the real monsters they were portraying hiding around the castle and even coming to visit them at night and scare the bejeezus out of them. The real monsters had come to see how they were being portrayed in the film, and they took a liking to the castle and its remote location. They let the film's actors and crew know that they wanted them to leave, and then they would make this their permanent home. If anyone tried to stop them or if the filming continued, all those involved would meet a fate worse than death."

Casey: "First, the actors portraying the monsters gave notice they were quitting. Then the production crew did the same."

Ole: "Weren't there contracts that would prohibit them from quitting?"

Lates: "There was. Thy told their agents, and their lawyers that they feared for their lives and no amount of money was worth dying for."

Doug: "The movie's director was in charge, and he was adamant that he would not let anyone out of their contract. If they continued to pursue litigation, he would make sure none of the actors or the crew would ever work in the movies again."

Pierce: "The actors and even some of the crew swore that the real counterparts to the characters they were hired to play continued to visit them at night or in dark recesses of the castle when no one else was around to see them. The actors begged and pleaded with the real monsters that they were being forced by the director and had no choice but to continue to fulfill their contracts and finish the movie."

Archie: "At first small accidents and equipment failures began to haunt the production. The real monsters had begun to sabotage the filming. Although the movies portrayed the monsters as heartless fiends, they were really just misunderstood beings who were outcasts from society. All they wanted was to be left alone with their own kind to live in peace."

Casey: "The director refused to stop production no matter what. Until that fateful day finally came."

Ole and I were now spellbound with anticipation. "What happened on the fateful day?" Asked Ole.

Lates: "It was a day when the sky was overcast with black clouds, a light drizzle came down from the sky and glistened deadly off the tower of the castle keep. Hanging by his neck from one of the towers' battlements was the movie's director. A chain was wrapped around his neck. Both of his eyes had been plucked from his face and placed between his teeth. Giving him an all-seeing smile for the world to see. Some would say he could now see the error of his ways right from the director's mouth. The arms and legs of his naked body were twisted and contorted into a shape that spelled out 'end'. He looked every bit the part of the monsters he was ignoring."

Doug: "Sure am glad I wasn't around to have to prepare that body for the hereafter."

Pierce: "To say the least, the production of the movie came to an immediate halt. The local constable said the case was well beyond his capabilities as there were far too many suspects. Scotland Yard sent its best detectives to investigate. Besides all the actors who were there to portray the monsters, there were ten times that many people working on the set. Many of them had come close to being injured or killed in the sets 'little' accidents. In the end, the story of the 'real' monsters taking over has been accepted by many as the truth."

Archie: "To this very day, it is said the 'real' monsters now live happily in the ruins of Longhall Castle."

Ole: "Did they ever catch the murderer?"

Casey: "It is still an unsolved mystery here in Longhall County and at Scotland Yard. Some believe it may have been one or any number of all the actors and film crew working together to rid themselves of the movie's director so they could leave and return safely to their loved ones and to their homes."

Lates: "Others believe it was the 'real' monsters that did away with the director. It would take someone or something of enormous strength to twist a man's limbs into the word 'end.'

Doug: "As for me. I don't think it was the 'real' monsters. They had more empathy than that. I think they are just misunderstood creatures who have been ostracized because they are different than us."

Pierce: "Wouldn't the 'real' monsters be guilty of murder by association if it was them that drove the actors and film crew to commit murder?"

Archie: "Pierce has a good point."

Ole: "Wait just a minute; you guys don't really believe there are 'real' monsters in the castle, do you?"

In unison, the group said, "Yes."

Ole: "Hold on. Let's just say they were 'real' monsters. You can't possibly believe they still live in the castle."

Casey: "There's a reason no one goes there anymore."

Ole: "Ok, so what you guys are telling me is that you believe the monsters are real and that, to this very day, they still inhabit the ruins of Longhall Castle?"

Once again, in unison, the group answered. "Yes."

Lates: "Ole, you need to remember the Longhall County motto. Where Legends live, and reality dies."

CHAPTER 9

We left the pub well after dark. The ride home was rather quiet, as I think both of us were contemplating the motto of Longhall County. 'Where Legends live, and reality dies.' What the heck is that all about? We had a feeling we were being duped. Probably just a cruel joke to play on the new Lord of the County. If that was the case, the residents had gone to extremes to pull it off. The boxing match, Paddington Bear and Indiana Jones. Then to top it all off was the story of the 'monsters 'of Longhall Castle.

Once we were back snug and comfortable in our cottage, we decided to make a 'to-do' list of things to see and places to visit in our county. We had heard that not far from our cottage was the Oast House, where the county's harvest of hops was grown, dried, mixed, fermented and kegged or bottled to become the local beverage of choice 'Hedgehog' beer.

The railway yards were, of course, on the top of the list for Ole. A visit to St. Catherine's church and its ages-old graveyard was another point of interest. The 'mine' on Longhall Mountain would certainly be of interest. The myriad of shops and businesses in the village needed exploration as time permitted. There was also the wharf and the riding stables, and farm. Of course, Longhall Castle and its keep would be a focal point to visit and would give us a vantage point at which we could survey most of the county. That would be best to do during daylight hours. Not that we are superstitious, mind you. Ok, maybe we are, just a bit. We might just put that one on the back burner until we learn more about the Longhall County moto.

While wandering around the county on our Norwegian Taxi, we noticed a high pinnacle of a building off in the distance, so we headed in that direction. We soon came to a building with a cylindrical tower on one end attached to a more conventional rectangular building on the opposite end. There was another smaller detached structure with two garage doors on one side and what looked to be a small office or living quarters on the far end. That building seemed to be a workshop, tractor shed or possibly horse stables. Fields filled with hops were located off in the distance.

A two-horse team hitched to a blue wagon with a load of hops and was being transferred to the main building. Near the tractor-horse shed was a man driving an older tractor pulling a trailer filled with wooden barrels. The yard around the area was filled with assorted sacks, barrels and miscellaneous tools that were scattered about along the walls of the buildings.

We pulled up near the tractor-horse shed, and then we walked over by the two men who were unloading hops from the wagon.

One of the men kept working, and the other one approached us. "What ye want. We ain't open to visitors, and we don't give out any free beer samples. Ye best be on your way."

Ole: "We were just hoping to look around a bit."

Man: "You're a Yank by your accent. Be on your way. Ye not welcome here."

Ole: "I'm just curious, is all. I don't want to intrude, but I happen to be related to Lord Long, and I am taking over for him since his demise. If I am correct in my assumption, this place is on Longhall County land, which means I have a direct concern about it. Not that I have any intention of changing anything; I was just hoping to see what this place is and what goes on here. You're right. I am a Yank, and I have never seen a building like this from where I come from back in the States. My name is Ole, and my canine partner is Tesse. We're glad to meet you."

Man: "So you're the new Lord Ole we've heard about. I guess you be welcome here, but you best talk to the owner to make sure. Ye ain't makin' no airs to me, but you'll find the owner around the corner of the shed over there. I best be back to work."

As we were walking towards the shed, I told Ole that the workers here didn't seem too friendly. He agreed but said it was probably not that unusual for them to be standoffish to strangers. Best to my knowledge, I believe those men were unloading hops to be used to make beer. In that case, and the fact that our friend there mentioned no free beer, I think it would be safe to say that we had stumbled on to the local brewery.

You know, if a place is part of Longhall County and included in our inheritance, maybe we could get them the recipe for SvenBrew, and they could add it to their product line. Ole smiled at me, and I could tell he had the same idea floating around in his head as I did.

Rounding the corner of the building, we saw a small section of the building jutting out from the main structure that blocked our view to the other side of it. We slowly walked around it and came face to face with a man sitting on an empty wooden keg of Hedgehog beer surrounded by empty beer bottles. He held a half-empty bottle of said beer in his hand, and he was swaying a bit to keep his balanced perch on the keg.

It took him a few moments for his eyes to focus on us. "Who are you, and what do you want? You don't like constables."

Ole introduced himself and me to the man.

Man: "So you're the new Lord of Longhall County. Figured you'd show up sooner or later. If you want to renegotiate my lease, you can forget it. I work hard, and I supply the best beer in the county. In fact, I supply the only beer made in Longhall County. You know how I know it's the best beer in the county?"

Ole: "Why?"

Man: "Because I make sure to sample every batch to make sure it's up to snuff. If you were wondering, this is what I'm doing right at this moment before I was so rudely interrupted."

Ole: "That's very commendable of you, sir. The Brew Master should sample his product to make sure it is up to his standards and the standards of his customers.

We are not here to renegotiate your lease. We saw your building from a distance, and we were curious as to what it was. Now that you know who we are, may I ask your name?"

Man: "They call me Whiskey Steve. Been the owner and Brew Master here for years, took it over from my father Wally, bless his poor departed soul." He hoped down from the barrel, and on wobbly legs, he shook Ole's hand and patted me on the head as Ole grabbed Steve's arm to help him regain his balance as he straightened up.

It now dawned on me that this was the same Whiskey Steve that we had received rude comments from on our first visit to Chaps Pub. If Ole recognized him, he did not let on, and I figured it best not to stir the pot by bringing up the past.

Steve: "I suppose you're wondering what I am doing back here. Well, I'll tell ya, but you need to keep it a secret just between us. It's the government and the aliens. They've both been trying to spy on me. Probably want the secret to my recipe for Hedgehog beer. I found this little corner where they couldn't see me and read my mind. Their satellites and drones can't penetrate the wall of this building, and they can't see 'round the corners, so I'm safe here. I think at this time of day it might be all right if I go out in the open for a bit. Would you like a tour of the place?"

Ole: "That would be much appreciated. We don't have places shaped like this back in the States."

Steve: "I believe these are exclusive to the British Isles. It's an Oast House. Another word for it would be a kiln for drying hops to make beer. We grow all our own hops. Then we dry them, and eventually, they are processed to brew our beer. If you go to any pub, tavern or liquor-serving establishment in Longhall County, you'll find that our Hedgehog beer is served there."

On the far side of the Oast House, there are vats for fermenting the beer. Once the fermentation is finished, it is run through a system of filters to remove any sediment. When that is done, it is put into kegs or bottles to be sold. We even have our own small bottling plant right here on site. We don't put any of our beer in cans. Sir Long himself made that decree years ago. He said putting beer in cans ruins the flavor, and it is the drink of drunkards and not fit for the fine people of Longhall County. It has one other advantage in that the bottles are reusable and good for the environment."

Once the tour of the Oast house was over, Steve took us to the tractor-horse shed. He explained that on one side of the shed was a small stable for the two workhorses, and the other side was used for maintenance of the tractor and farm machinery.

On the end of the shed was a small enclosure where Steve lived. He invited us in, and it was well-lived in and a bit on the messy side. He brushed some girlie magazines off the couch and invited us to have a seat. He handed Ole a bottle of beer and then opened one that he poured into a bowl for me. Of course, he also opened a beer for himself.

Steve: "You don't plan on changing things around her, do you?"

Ole: "We've just arrived. As far as changing things, we hope to be able to leave everything as it is. At least for now. In the future, if we see something that might benefit the community, then maybe we can discuss changes at that time. As far as Tesse and I can tell, this place is fine just the way it is. Unless, of course, you are worried about the aliens taking over. I assume you're talking about aliens from other countries? If so, I can assure you that I am not in favor of opening the boundaries of Longhall County to foreigners or illegal aliens."

Steve: "You're a foreigner. A Yank form the colonies. Seems to me you're taking over."

Ole: "Not taking over, just overseeing as my great-grandfather did. True, I am a foreigner. But I am of the same bloodline as my great-grandfather, and I am next in line to resume his legacy. I believe it makes me a citizen of Longhall County legally, even if it is by default."

Steve: "So be it. Best we keep the foreigners out. Now we just have to worry about the aliens. I'm talking about aliens from outer space, mind you. You know they have bases here on Earth. They set them up in big bio-domes under the oceans and seas. They like to come out and take over people's minds and bodies, just like in that old movie The Pod People.

It should be obvious that they have been taking over the government and the media. It was them that developed all these computers and things that people put in their homes so that they could spy on us. The devil's instruments are used by aliens if you ask me. In fact, maybe they are devils from outer space. The Bible says he cast them from his midst to the earth. So they are probably just creatures from other planets. Look at how they changed the laws to favor the minority people over the majority of hard-working tax paying citizens. It will just be a matter of time before they take over the whole world.

That's why we folks in Longhall County want to keep things as they are. We live in our own little world and don't want any outsiders to interfere. Sure, some of the folks around here have cell phones and computers, but you'll not find any around here. I don't believe in them. Won't have those little green-eyed buggar's from outer space or the government spy on me.

Let the outsiders have their multiple sexes and global warming. We folks in Longhall have God's Ten Commandants and the bible. We got only two sexes, and we respect each other. As for that global warming crap, the world's been changing since its inception. That's how God designed it, and ain't nothing mankind can do to change that. These liberals think they can hold back the ocean tides and that cow farts are going to change the atmosphere. The Bible says we could eat meat, so let them vegan people graze in the fields just so long as they ain't eating my hops and moving into our county. I'll let them be."

That was a mouthful, and Steve made a few good points as far as Ole and I were concerned. However, we figured a bit too much beer might have pickled his brain a bit. Or maybe it was the beer and the combination of fermenting hop fumes from the brewery.

Ole: "Steve, I'm curious; you brew and drink beer, but you said they call you Whiskey Steve. How come?"

Steve seemed to get a bit fidgety at that question. "Let's just say the man does not live by beer alone. I really need to get back to my safe place. You can never be sure when someone might be watching you."

We followed him out of his living quarters, and he bee-lined his way back to his perch around the corner. As we drove away, I looked at Ole and said. "He's a bit strange."

Ole: "That he is. But it was an interesting tour, and I enjoyed it. I can also say I found him a rather unique individual."

"Yes, he is." Said I.

It was lunchtime, so we headed into the village for a bite to eat. Next to the Hedgehoghaven train station was the Bulldog Café. It aroused our curiosity when we saw it from our coach window when we first arrived at the village. It was unique in that the building was actually shaped like a big white bulldog. Ole mentioned that it was reminiscent of the novelty-shaped buildings that were popular tourist places in the States during the heyday of highway building programs in the 1950s to 1960s era.

It was a small place about the size of Rocky's Tavern. On one side of the building facing the train station, was a take-out window for those in a hurry or wanting a bite to eat while waiting for the next train. We decided to park in the lot near the café and walk over for a sit-down meal.

There were two men standing outside the café. Both were dressed in what one would describe as 'space' suits with rocket packs on their backs. I looked at Ole and said. "Remember when I told you about Paddington Bear being at the railway station? Well, if I'm not mistaken, those two look just like the Rocketeer from the movie of the same name, and the other one sure does look like Buzz Lightyear from the Toy Story movie. One is a human, and the other is a cartoon character. So now what do you have to say about my seeing Paddington Bear?"

Ole kept quiet as we passed the two men; we sort of eavesdropped on their conversation as we slowly walked by them, doing our best not to try and stare. From what we heard, they were discussing the pros and cons of their rocket-powered backpacks.

Ole: "Yeah, Paddington Bear. Maybe we best remember the Longhall County moto. Where Legends live, and reality dies."

Once inside, we were greeted by the two owners. Twin sisters Elanor and Rosey. In unison, they greeted us. "Afternoon, sir and canine. May we suggest our world-famous third-pound Bulldog Burger and fries? Possibly a nice chocolate milkshake as the 'piece de resistance' to top it off."

Ole: "Sounds great. We'll take two."

Elanor: "I'm Elanor the chief cook and bottle washer. That's my sister Rosey, an order taker and bus lady. Might I assume by your accent that you are the new Lord of the County? Lord Ole and Tesse, I believe."

Ole: "We are. Nice to meet you. I love your building. Gives me a nostalgic feeling of home from when I was a kid back in the States.

Rosey: "Thank you. We got the idea from a book of unusual buildings in the colonies, and it started me thinking that Hedgehoghaven needed a unique eating establishment that would be one of the first things people would see when they arrived by train. When I was watching the movie Rocketeer, I just knew I had to have a café similar to the one in the movie. My contractors thought I was crazy, but they did as I asked, and it turned out to be the talk of the county."

Ole: "I remember that movie; it was great. In fact, speaking of the movies. Tesse and I just saw someone out in front of your place that looked just like the Rocketeer from the movie. We could also swear that he was talking to Buzz Lightyear from the movie Toy Story."

Elanor: "Oh yeah, those two. They're regulars in here. All they ever want to talk about is jet packs and rocket propulsion. I like them both, but all that talk of flying around with just their jet packs gets old after a while. They keep threatening to have an air race around the village someday. I don't know if it will ever happen, though. If they did and one of them lost to the other, well, it might just ruin a good friendship."

Ole: "That surely would draw a crowd. But I see what you mean; it wouldn't be worth losing their friendship over a race."

The Bulldog Burger was a bit undercooked for Ole's taste, but I thought it was great. We finished off our meal, thanked our host, and we went back on the road. "Where next?" I asked.

Ole: "I was thinking we ought to swing over to the railroad shops and check them out."

I should have known better than to ask. Ole was dying to go there even though he tried to make it sound as if it was no big deal. I knew that this was going to be the highlight of his day. He loved trains. A Hedgehog beer at the Oast House or a Bulldog Burger at the Bulldog Café would pale in comparison to the smells and sounds of a vintage steam locomotive.

We pulled into the railway yards, and Ole just sat on the scooter for a while, taking in the sights and smells of steam, oil and coal that permeated our nostrils. He finally pulled out his cell phone 'the devil's instrument, according to Whiskey Steve and started taking pictures.

There were two engine houses for repairs and maintenance. It was easy to see that one had been there much longer than the other one, which most likely was added as the shops expanded. The older of the two shops had its own water tower, a small stone storage shed and a coal bunker. At the side of the building was a loading ramp that had an old steam tractor, forklift and a track-driven crane that had been salvaged from the Hedgehoghaven wharf that replaced with a larger, more modern apparatus.

The newer of the two shops had its own water tower that serviced it and storage a track that veered off to the side. The newer shop was empty, but the older shop, which was larger and looked to be better equipped to handle larger jobs, tempted us with just the front end of a locomotive being visible.

We got off our taxi and started to wander around. There were a number of employees working in the area, but they didn't seem to take any notice of us. The men at work were busy welding, moving sleepers and hauling various parts to and fro. If we had been back in the States roaming around on our own like this, a railroad policeman would have grabbed us by the scruff of the neck and unceremoniously tossed us off of the property on our duffs.

All of a sudden, we were approached by a man in a denim shirt with his name 'Roger' embroidered above the front pocket. The back of the shirt was also hand embroidered with a steam locomotive, and in a half circle above and below the locomotive, it read "Hedgehoghaven Railway.' He had seen us from the window of the Crossing Keepers Cottage, which served as his home and his office.

He was of average height, thinning wavy blonde hair and of average build. He introduced himself as the shop's manager and asked if he could help us.

Ole told him we were railroad enthusiasts and reluctantly added that he was the new Lord of Longhall County.

Roger: "So you're the ones our little pug engine was shuttling around a while back."

Ole: "That was us. I got some great pictures of that little 0-4-0 pug. What a great little locomotive."

Roger: "Good thing you got pictures when you did. The pug will be getting pulled from service soon. It's in need of a rebuild. Besides, the pug just wasn't able to handle some of the larger loads that it needed to pull. We'll be bringing in a 0-6-0 tank engine that used to run on the Great Northern Railway. It has been in offsite storage, and it's shopped and ready for service. Sir Long insisted that any locomotives we run here be kept in their original livery and with original numbers. This one retains the engine number 1247 and its original green livery paint scheme. You'll like her she's a beauty.

Ole: "I'm amazed that you still run steam locomotives and vintage four-wheel train cars."

Roger: "Train cars? Oh, you mean wagons. We call them 'wagons' here in England as far as running steam locomotives and vintage wagons, that is in the Longhall County charter. It seems that the Long and Hall families liked the way things were in the past, so they have done all they can to keep it that way. Of course, some of the more modern amenities have slipped in here and there. We now have cell phones, computers and even satellite television. Gasoline and diesel vehicles are allowed, but absolutely none of those newfangled electric cars will ever be allowed in our county."

One of the last purchases your great-grandfather made before he passed away is in the number one shed undergoing a final check over before it is to be put into service. Would you like to see it?"

That was a silly question to ask Ole. He, of course, jumped at the chance.

We walked into the shop with its smell of grease, oil and steam permeating our nostrils. Right in front of us, in its splendid red livery, sat the #5972 Hogwarts Castle 4-6-0 locomotive.

Ole: "I've read all the Harry Potter books and Tesse, and I have seen all the movies. We never dreamed this locomotive actually existed."

Roger: "Not only does it exist but on the day of its inaugural run Harry Potter, Hermione Granger, and Ron Weasley will be here to officiate."

I whispered to Ole. "Where Legends live, and reality dies."

Roger: "Well, there you are. Welcome to my world. We could have gotten the passenger coaches to go with it, but Sir Long's rules limit our railroad to four-wheel coaches only. Although there is a rumor that shortly before he passed away, he might have made a change to the rules that would allow vintage six-wheel coaches in the future."

Ole shook Roger's hand and thanked him for his hospitality. I got a goodbye pat on the head from Roger as we turned to leave.

We had done enough exploring for one day and went home to have some supper and relax. Ole made us clam strips in the air-fryer that was part of our kitchen appliance selection.

We sat down and decided to watch the movie Fantastic Beasts and Where to find them. Ole mentioned how impressed he was with J.K. Rowling's Harry Potter books.

He said that when they were in their heyday, he would see people reading them in restaurants as he was doing himself. Often times when these readers noticed each other, they would quickly discuss the books amongst themselves. Not only that, but the readers covered all ages, from young to old. She had created a phenomenon where all of a sudden, it became popular for everyone to admit that they enjoyed reading a book. Something very lacking in this day and age of cell phones and computers. As for Ole, he loves to read, and I love to listen to him read. Books open up a whole new world for the two of us much like Hedgehoghaven is doing for us right now.

CHAPTER 10

We spent the next few weeks doing some things around our cottage. Occasionally we would drive into the village for a meal and to check out the local businesses. Slowly but surely, we were getting acquainted with more and more of the locals.

We received an invitation to attend a meeting at Chaps, so we made our way to the village at the appointed time. We were surprised to see the Ecto-1 ambulance from the original Ghostbusters movie parked on the street near Chaps Pub.

Ole pulled the Norwegian Taxi to the side of the road, and he was taking his cell phone from his belt holster before his feet touched the ground. He ran over to the Ecto-1 and was busy snapping pictures. "This is fantastic. The only thing that could top this is if the original Ghostbusters were here with it."

I just gave a tail-wagging smile at my partner's antics and looked around to see how many people were watching him embarrass himself.

We had to walk around a blue police box as we made our way to Chaps. I thought it was a rather unusual place for a police box and had never noticed it on our previous visits to the pub.

We entered the pub, and it was rather busy for being so early in the day. A few of the tables had been pushed together to accommodate the eight people that were seated around them. Most noticeable by the description we had heard of him was Chief Constable Pete. Being about two meters tall and tipping the scale at 159 kilograms.

There were four men in tan coveralls that were none other than the original Ghostbusters. Peter Venkman, Ray Stanz, Egon Spengler and Winston Zeddmore. There were three others that we did not immediately recognize. We went to the bar to see what was going on.

It was still a bit early for us to want a beer, so Ole asked Casey for a bottle of Mountain Dew and a bowl of milk for me.

Ole: "What's with the big pow-wow over there? I recognize the Ghostbusters and Constable Pete, but I don't believe I know the other gentlemen. I saw the Ecto-1 outside; you got ghosts in your pub?"

Casey: "This is England, and our village is quite old, so of course there are ghosts, just none in my place as far as I know. However, you can never be sure. It's always possible that you might do something to disturb them, and then they might just pop up anywhere."

As for the pow-wow you asked about, I assume that's an American colloquialism for a gathering or a meeting. I believe they sent you an invitation to attend. Deacon Carl is the instigator. Seems he is getting fed up with not only his parishioners but now the Sunday school class of kids asking about monsters or ghosts at Longhall Castle. So he asked the Ghostbusters, Dr. Who and Sherlock Holmes to come here and investigate the matter. You best hustle over there, as I believe they are waiting for you."

Ole and I made our way over to the meeting where we were asked to take a seat. It was a bit crowded, so I sat on Ole's lap. Introductions were made, and the meeting was called to order, with Deacon Carl acting as the chairman.

Carl: "I sent each of you a letter of invitation to come here to discuss the matter of the monsters or ghosts that are rumored to be living in Longhall Castle. It was not doing much harm when the folks at the pubs would tell their stories about seeing ghosts or monsters at the castle. What worries me now is that the kids in my Sunday school classes are talking about going to the castle to see for themselves.

As all of us know, the castle is a dangerous, crumbling old ruin, and it is not safe for anyone to go exploring around it. So once and for all, I was hoping that between Sherlock Holmes, Dr. Who and the Ghostbusters, one or all of you would investigate the ruins of the castle and dispel the rumors of there being any monsters or ghosts living or, I guess that might be un-living in the case of ghosts at the castle."

Sherlock: "Deacon, just what exactly do you mean by monsters?"

Carl: "There have been stories that years ago a movie studio unwittingly unleashed the real Frankenstein monster and his bride, Dracula, Wolfman, Mummy and the Gill Man from the Black Lagoon from wherever they had been hiding to their new home at Longhall Castle. As for ghosts, this is England. There are always stories of ghosts, so that part does not bother me as much as the fact that there may actually be real monsters there."

Sherlock stood up and put on his coat and hat as he prepared to leave. He then gave his explanation. "Any logical person with an inkling of education knows that ghosts and the monsters you are talking about are strictly fictional. I deal in reality. You have wasted my time, so I will be taking my leave."

We watched Sherlock walk out of the door as Egon made a comment. "Well, I, for one, am glad that Sherlock Holmes has left. He sure did discount what we Ghostbusters do for a living."

Peter: "Educated idiot is what I think of him."

Ray: "The man is entitled to his opinion."

Winston: "He is, even if he is wrong."

Dr. Who: "I've been all over the universe, so I have no doubts that there may be ghosts and even monsters. I'm not so sure that the particular monsters you are talking about exist. I must say that I do find it an intriguing possibility. However, there is a Dalek problem that takes precedence for me at this time, so I think I'll take my leave and let the Ghostbusters handle this one."

Peter: "Great. We have the field all to ourselves."

Egon: "Not so fast, Peter. We specialize in ghosts, not monsters.

Ray: "Slimmer was a ghost but also sort of a monster."

Winston: "There's a difference. Slimmer was a ghost and not a flesh-and-blood monster. Our proton packs and neutron wands can suck up a ghost. I don't think they'll do us much good against real flesh and blood monsters."

Peter: "I say let's do it. What have we got to lose? If it's ghosts, we'll get them."

Winston: "If it's monsters, I vote we run like hell."

The four of them got up from their chairs and headed out the door. We heard the wailing of the Ecto-1 siren as it sped off towards Longhall Castle.

As the siren faded into the distance, a man came into the pub dressed in a fireman's outfit. He looked around and saw us, so he decided to join in. He came to our table and introduced himself to me as Dale, the Chief of the fire department. He asked what the siren was all about. Pete gave him a quick rundown of what had just transpired. Explaining that Sherlock Holmes had turned us down. Dr. Who had more pressing matters to deal with. Yet, the Ghostbusters had agreed to take the job.

Dale: "Carl, you actually asked those people to come here over a few ghosts. If I was you, I'd be more concerned with the ghosts at St. Catherine's instead of those at the castle."

Carl: "There are no ghosts at St. Catherine's. Even if there was, I'm more concerned about the village kids going to look for ghosts and monsters at the castle. If I can assure them there are no ghosts or monsters there, maybe they will forget about exploring the castle and possibly getting hurt. Those old ruins are a dangerous place for anyone to be around."

Pete: "I tend to agree with Carl about the Ghostbusters. I'd hate to see some kids wander up there and get hurt. Although Dale also has a point. Maybe when the Ghostbusters are done checking out the castle, you should have them do a sweep of St. Catherine's. I've been on night patrol, and I've heard some strange sounds coming from either the graveyard or the church."

Dale: "I've heard the same sounds myself when I've been on the night shift at the fire station. Sounded like moaning and groaning to me."

Pete: "Plus an occasional scream now and then as if someone was in agony."

Carl: "What may or may not be in St. Catherine's is none of your concern. I best get back to my duties. We'll hopefully see all of you at Sunday services."

Ole: "I know I'm new here and a bit of an outsider, but shouldn't things like hiring people to take care of ghosts be brought up at a village meeting? Especially if we are paying them from the village coffers."

Pete: "It should, but Carl gets carried away when it comes to protecting the children of the village."

Dale: "You can't fault him for that. After all, the kids are the future of Longhall County."

Ole: "So the village will pay for it?"

Pete: "It will come out of the county expense account."

Dale: "You can bet when word comes around that it will also come out of donations to St. Catherine's. Folks will hold back a bit of the church's donations figuring the church wanted to hire the Ghostbusters, so by holding back, they'll make sure the church pays for most of the expense. You can bet Carl won't like that, and he'll think twice before pulling another stunt like this."

Ole: "What would happen if the Ghostbusters actually find ghosts?"

Pete: "Beats me."

Dale: "Me too."

Ole: "What if they find the monsters?"

Dale: "Then we know the old stories are true. Although if they do find ghosts, I hope they don't catch any of them."

Ole: "Why not?"

Pete: "This is England. What would England be without its ghosts?"

Ole: "In other words, it will be like the county motto. Legends live, and reality dies."

Dale: "Exactly."

We mentioned that we were going over to Olive's café for breakfast. Dale asked if he might accompany us. We invited him along, figuring it would be a good thing to get to know as many of the locals as possible.

Olive made us blueberry pancakes, hash browns and bacon, along with orange juice for Ole and milk for me. Dale copied Ole's order but substituted coffee instead of orange juice.

Dale: "So, what do you think of our little village so far?"

Ole: "We like it here. Some of the things we've seen seem sort of strange to us. I suppose the County moto has something to do with that."

Dale: "I can see that you might get a bit confused. You'll get used to it over time."

Ole: "What do you think will happen if the Ghostbusters find monsters instead of ghosts?"

Dale: "I think they'll high tail it out of the County, and then we won't have to pay them anything. That would probably make everyone happy except for Deacon Carl."

Ole: "About Deacon Carl. Were you and Pete serious about hearing noises at night coming from St. Catherine's?"

Dale: "We were. Sometimes at night, Pete would stop by the fire station when I was on duty, and we'd stand near the graveyard and listen. I don't know if it was ghosts or not, but there were some eerie sounds coming from either the graveyard or the church. Almost sounded like a woman in agony."

Best not to mention it to the Ghostbusters. England is known for its many ghosts, and if the Ghostbusters started rounding them up, well, England just wouldn't be England without its ghosts."

We finished our breakfast and thanked Dale for joining us. "Where you off to now?" He asked.

Ole: "I think we might swing by the stables at the edge of town."

Dale: "You mean Carol's Stables. She's not around right now. However, she has someone running it for her in her absence. You'll get a surprise at who's in charge" He looked over at Olive, who had overheard our conversation, and they both laughed out loud.

As we left, I asked Ole what was so funny about the people that were running the stables but he was as much in the dark about it as I was. The best way to find out was to go and see for ourselves.

We drove over to the stables. The entrance was a two-part building with an open arched center large enough to accommodate a good-sized vehicle. Above the arch was a sign, 'Carol's Stables.' Out front, the stable was busy with activity. A horse-drawn hearse was practicing for its next funeral procession. A very fancy open carriage carrying a loving couple was practicing for a wedding procession. Certainly, there could have been no greater opposites out practicing on the same day.

Two riders dressed in scarlet red jackets and white pants, looking like a picture-perfect set of fox hunters, were riding two beautifully groomed horses. There were about a half-dozen other riders roaming about on joy rides.

We decided, for the safety of the horses, riders, and ourselves, to park away from all the activity. We walked through the arched entrance into an open courtyard. A lady was leading three ponies with young children on them as she taught them the basics of horsemanship.

The main house stood off to the far side and butted up to the seashore at the back. Near a workshop, a man was holding a horse still as a blacksmith fitted it with new shoes. The workshop had a stairway leading to the second floor, which we assumed was for employee housing.

A good distance from the main area was a pig sty with a number of pigs, including a sow with her newborn piglets.

A bit farther down was a stone wall corral with seven horses, one buffalo and a milk cow. Two people were sitting on the wall watching the horses when they noticed us. They jumped off the wall and came to greet us.

The man was tall and lanky. He wore a brown cowboy hat, red bandana, tan shirt, a white vest with black spots, blue jeans and brown boots. The girl was slim with a red hat, white vest with yellow trim and flowers across the front, a sash with white chaps and black spots covering the front of her blue jeans, and brown boots completed her outfit.

I looked at Ole and said. "Do you know who those two are?"

I recognize the man. That's Woody from Toy Story. The other one is his girlfriend, but for the life of me, I can't remember her name."

"It's Jesse. This is great. I can't believe it's really them. I love Toy Story."

Woody and Jesse walked over to greet us and introduced themselves. Jesse picked me up and cuddled me to her chest, telling me what a beautiful girl I was as Woody shook Ole's hand. Needless to say, I liked Jesse a lot.

They explained that Carol was away and they were temporarily in charge of the stables. At this time, they were not sure when or if Carol would ever return.

Ole: "That sounds a bit ominous."

Woody: "It does, and it doesn't. That's all we know. So, we are in charge for however long it takes."

Jesse: "Yes, siree. Just me and Woody doing what we love. Taking care of horses and the other animals and teaching kids to ride. What a great job. We don't care if Carol ever returns. Do we, Woody?"

Woody: "Well, I wouldn't exactly say that. This is her place, so we do hope she decides to come back. In the meantime, how would you two like a two-bit tour of the place?"

Jesse: "Get it. Two-bit as in horse bit. My Woody is so funny."

Woody: "Or it will cost you two bits as in twenty-five cents."

Jesse: "I told you he was funny; gotta remember, we're from the United States, so we still talk in dollars and cents. No pounds or quid or shillings or whatever else they call their money over here."

We were shown the workshops, pig sty, the employees living quarters and horse stalls that were up to the standards of the best stables in England, according to Jesse.

The main house was off-limits until Carol returned except to Jesse and Woody, who were occupying it while they were in charge. As we walked around, we passed a tall, lanky American-looking cowboy on a white horse. A shorter man on what looked to be a Norwegian fjord horse rode beside him. Both of them looked familiar, so once they were out of hearing range, I told Ole to ask who they were.

Woody: "The cowboy is Lucky Luke, and his horse is Jolly Jumper. You would have to read some Belgian comics by a man named Morris to learn more about them. Even though the writer is Belgian, the exploits of those two are very American."

Jesse: "American, just like Woody and me. Genuine cowboy and cowgirl. Right Woody?"

Woody: "Right, Jesse. The shorter fellow is Tyrion Lannister riding a Norwegian fjord horse that he keeps here. You've probably seen him in the television series Game of Thrones.

With the tour finished, we thanked our hosts and went along our way. The uncertainty about the stable's owner seemed a bit sad. However, the place seemed to be in good hands with

Woody and Jesse. Between meeting them and seeing Lucky Luke, Jolly Jumper, and Tyrion Lannister, the County moto was holding true. Where Legends live, and reality dies.

I hopped into the sidecar and heard Ole unhappily say. "Oh poop, darn son- of –a-gun."

"Oh poop, darn, son–of–a–gun what?" I asked.

Ole: I just stepped into a pile of horse sh…"

"Shh, no swearing. There are other people in earshot. I gave a tail-wagging laugh as Ole lifted his foot to reveal its new soft, smelly brown coating of, well, you know, horse poop.

He took off his shoe and walked over to a grassy spot to wipe it off on the grass as best he could. Then he made his way along a path that led down to the sea and swished his shoe in the water until it was free of that 'stuff.' I heard him squish-squish his way back to me with a wet shoe on one foot. He looked at me and said. "Don't you dare say anything, or I'll toss you into a pile of horse manure to see how you like it? My shoe will dry as we ride along in the wind."

Ole's little misstep put him temporally in a bad mood, but he did his best not to let it dampen his spirit. Get it? 'Dampen' like his wet shoe. We continued on with our day of exploration, heading west along the seashore until we came to the Hedgehoghaven Wharf.

The wharf was even more active than the stables had been. We parked near a food truck called the 'Frying Fish.' It was lunchtime so guess what Ole and I had for dinner. We found an empty spot on the docks to sit as we watched the activity taking place on the water.

There was a freighter being unloaded with a gantry crane on the wharf. The 'Luda Times' canal boat with its bright blue paint job was passing by with some tourists on board. Two fishing boats, the 'Olivia' and the 'Victoria' were heading out to sea. The steam-powered 'Africa Queen' was moored near the shore. Slowly chugging along was the puffer 'Carolsea', which was skippered by none other than Captain Pierce. As it passed us, we waved, and to our surprise, two individuals on deck waved back at us. They looked very much like Captain Jack Sparrow and Davy Jones. Ole and I looked at each other as we both mouthed the words. Where Legends live, and reality dies.

Once we had finished our meals, we decided to take a stroll along the wharf. We left our perch on the dock and started walking up a ramp that led to the wharf.

At the bottom of the ramp was a fishmonger selling fresh fish. His table was surrounded by wood crates filled with ice and an assorted catch of the day's fresh fish. Pelicans were perched nearby, waiting for leftovers that he would toss whenever he sold a fish and the customer wanted it cleaned. Seagulls were busy picking up scraps from the ground, and he had to occasionally shoo them away from his cutting table.

Walking up the ramp, we could see stacks of goods in wooden crates and barrels waiting their turn to be loaded or unloaded, as the case may be. Two men near the crates seemed to be arguing about a skinny woman with dark hair in a bun that stood near them. Her squeaking voice grated on our ears as she pleaded for the two men to calm down and quit arguing. Finally, the bigger of the two men grabbed the little man by the shirt and lifted him off the ground before tossing him into a stack of wooden crates. One of the crates broke open and the little man fell on top of it. The broken crate disgorged its contents of spinach. The little man's mouth had been open, and some of the spinach fell into it. He chewed up the spinach, swallowed it, and his muscles bulged as he jumped to his feet and walked over to the big man. The little fellow wound up his arm like a spinning airplane propeller as he made a fist and gave the big man an uppercut to his chin and sent him flying off the wharf. The woman ran to the little man and hugged him. I could swear we saw little hearts of love floating off of them and into the air.

I said to Ole. "Did you see that?"

Ole: "I did. You know who they are, don't you? Or was it before your time?"

"I'm afraid I don't. Must be before my time. Who are they?"

Ole: "That's Popeye, Brutus and Olive Oyl. When Popeye eats spinach, he gets super–human strength."

"You mean like Superman?"

Ole: "Sort of, but he can't fly or leap over tall buildings."

A bit farther down the docks was a Royal Navy motorcycle with a sidecar. An officer and a seaman were both in dress white and seemed to be assessing the area. We weren't exactly sure what they were doing, but in this age of turmoil and trouble all over the world, it could be anyone's guess. It was possible that they were making sure the docking areas and wharfs in England were safe and secure, just in case.

We passed by a lot of seamen and dock workers. Some were just lolling about, and others were hard at work. Occasionally we had to step aside to avoid being run over by the forklift that was moving things about. Crates and barrels of goods seemed to be stacked about everywhere we looked. There was no doubt that the Hedgehoghaven Wharf was doing a brisk business.

We located a couple of wood barrels that were out of the way of all the hubbub and spent a couple of enjoyable hours watching the unloading of a freighter that was moored to the docks. Once, I glanced down along what we knew as cattails, but the British refer to them as bulrushes. I could have sworn I saw a gilled creature the size of a man slipping away into the area near them. I told Ole to look, but it was too late. The creature was gone. Ole figured I was seeing things. My imagination conjured up images of the Gill Man from the movie Creature from the Black Lagoon. Although from the local legends we had heard, the Gill Man was supposedly living at Longhall Castle. In my mind, that did not make much sense. It was much more logical that he would be living near the water. So maybe I really did see him.

As we were heading home, we stopped at the Phillips 66 gas station next to Olive's Café. It was a tiny A-frame building made of stone and painted red with white trim. A steel cart with four pumps of assorted grades of oil sat near the door. For gas, there were two old-style gravity pumps with tall glass globes on their tops. Unlike Tony's Repair, this place was strictly for selling gasoline and not for doing service or repair work. From the looks of the place, it would have been at home in the 1920s to early 1940s America.

It had been a fun and adventurous day, and we went home happy and content with our day's discoveries.

HEDGEHOGHAVEN

CHAPTER 11

We settled in for movie night with homemade sugar popcorn that Ole made from his mom's old family recipe. If you've never heard of it, think of caramel popcorn without the caramel.

Ole showed up with our popcorn, a bowl of water for me, and a bottle of A&W root beer for him. "What we watching?" He asked.

"The original 1954 Creature from the Black Lagoon."

Ole: "Really? I suppose you picked that out because you thought you saw the 'Gill Man' by the wharf."

"I don't think I saw him. I did see him. So stick your fingers in your popcorn bowl and eat it."

Ole: "Well, aren't we a bit touchy tonight? To take your mind off the Gill Man and monsters, I think maybe tomorrow we will go and visit the mine just down the rails from here. Who knows, maybe the 'Mole Men' will be there."

I ignored his last comment. After the movie, we went to bed. Ole had to wake me up a couple of times during the night as I was whining and softly barking in my sleep. Best I could remember, I was either being threatened, or I was chasing away monsters from Ole and me.

We visited Chaps the day after the Ghostbusters went on their quest to locate any ghosts or monsters that might be residing at Longhall Castle. Deacon Carl was sitting at the bar nursing a pint of beer and looking rather dejected. Ole and I took a seat on either side of him.

Ole: "Carl, a bit early in the day to be drinking. Anything wrong?"

Carl: "Wrong? Of course not. That is if you have just been told the Ghostbusters left the area because they only hunt and capture ghosts and not real live monsters."

Casey: "Yes, sir. You heard it at Chaps first. Right before close last night, the Ecto-1 pulled up outside. Peter Venkman came in and grabbed some beer to go. Then he said they didn't see any ghosts, but sure as hell, they saw Dracula and Frankenstein's monster, who told them to clear out, or they would turn the Ghostbusters into ghosts, and they could then hunt themselves. Seems that they decided to return to the Colonies as it was safer to hunt ghosts there then it was here in England. It seems the Colonies would prefer to have their ghosts vanquished, unlike England, where we embrace them as part of our heritage."

Carl: "Now, what am I supposed to tell the children of the village? No kids, don't go roaming around the ruins of the castle as there are real live monsters up there. You know how kids are. You tell them something like that, and the first thing they will do is to go there to see for themselves."

Ole: "Of course you're right. That's how kids are. Maybe if Constable Pete was to talk to the kids, they might listen to him."

Carl: "If Pete gets involved, it will just be worse. Kids don't listen to the law nowadays. You own the castle. You should tear it down or at least fence it off so no one can go near it."

Casey: "You can't tear it down. It's a historical site. The only way a fence would stop anyone was if it was electrified. Frying kids on an electric fence would probably not go over very well with their parents."

Ole: "Fried kids might make a tasty morsel for the monsters."

Carl: "Interesting idea, but not practical. I guess the only answer is for Lord Ole to go to the castle and talk with the monsters. Convince them to move somewhere else or at least stay out of sight and not scare anyone. Especially the children. If they see any kids, they should hide from them."

Ole, Casey, and I, with a tail wagging, all laughed at Carl's last statement.

Ole: "First off, I doubt if anything I could say would cause monsters to hide from children or anyone else for that matter. Second, if there really are monsters in the castle, I'm not going to be dumb enough to approach them or talk to them. I may be from what you call the 'Colonies,' but that doesn't mean I'm crazy enough to go up against real monsters. I've seen all the old movies, and I've loved them. However, if those creatures are real, I prefer to see them on the movie screen or television and not face to face. You're almost a priest; maybe you should go and talk to them. They might listen to a man of God."

Casey: "Or you can exorcise them. Priests can do that, can't they?"

Carl: "Some Priests can. But I'm not a Priest, just a Deacon. Deacons don't wield much power in the church, and we sure don't have the ability to exorcise demons. Anyway, these aren't demons; they're monsters. Maybe if we all ignore it and not talk about it, the kids will lose their interest in monsters and find other things to talk about."

Casey: "Sounds like a plan to me. My kids never stayed on one subject too long. How about another beer Carl?"

Carl: "Sure, why not."

Ole: "Dale and Pete said they heard strange noises coming from St. Catherine's. Maybe you could let the kids investigate that to give them something to do."

Carl gave us a look that would have scared the devil himself. Then he took a big swig of his beer before talking. "I don't think that was an appropriate comment. St. Catherine's is not haunted."

Casey: "Carl, don't get your knickers in a bunch. Ole was just teasing you. Anyways, this is England. It's not that unusual to have a haunted church or graveyard."

About this time, we were joined at the bar by Archie, the owner of the local bakery. He ordered a beer and some pretzels. He took his false teeth from his mouth and dropped them into his glass of beer before he took a long swig of his now-smiling glass of liquid refreshment.

Archie gave a mischievous toothless smile as he spoke to Carl. "Hey Carl, I saw you talking to Marilyn Monroe in front of the church. Were you thinking about her for your new organist?"

That question, of course, got a snicker from all of us.

At first, Carl had not caught the risqué meaning attached to that statement until he saw the look on our faces.

Carl: "Archie, contrary to your rather vulgar comment, she is being considered for the position. I looked over her resume."

Archie butted in with. "I bet you did. What a resume she has. I noticed two of her qualifications right away."

Carl did his best to ignore Archie as a blush came to his cheeks. "As I was saying before, I was so rudely interrupted. Her resume is quite impressive. She has experience in singing and in playing the organ."

Our conversation was overheard by everyone in the pub, and the laughter that now erupted was impossible to ignore.

However, Carl did his best to ignore Archie and seriously continue on. "As I said, she has the experience to do the job. With the passing of our old organist, we need a replacement. As of this time, Miss Monroe is the only applicant. So I'll be giving her a try. I am sure she will be a welcome addition to St. Catherine's."

Archie: "You give her a try, Carl. Let us know how that works out for you. If nothing else, I bet she will help to increase the male attendance at Sunday services. I know I, for one, will be there from now on."

Carl: "Archie, why don't you put your teeth in your mouth backwards and eat those blasphemous words that just came out of your mouth."

That comment had everyone in the place laughing so hard that some of them were almost falling off their chairs. Even though Archie was the butt of the comment, he also found the remark worth a laugh as he replied. "You got me their Deacon. In my book, you're all right for a holy man."

Before anything else was said, Winton from 'In Cod, we Trust' and Ray, the owner of 'Lovett's Lamb and Meat shop,' walked in. They immediately joined us at the bar. Being regular Casey had two pints of beer ready and waiting for them before they were even seated.

Casey figured it was best to move the conversation away from Carl and Archie, so he asked the newest members of our group. "How was the fishing today, boys?"

Ray: "Great. We got the old Africa Queen running yesterday and took it out on its maiden voyage today."

Winton: "We were up at the crack of dawn this morning to get her boiler stoked up. She's a bit more work than a gas powered boat but she makes you feel like a real old time sailor."

Ray: "Other than the slap of her gear rod to the propeller shaft, she's also much quieter than a gas-powered engine."

Winton: "Makes it easier to sneak up on the fish."

Ray: "Winton, tell everyone what you think you saw today."

Winton: "I don't think I saw it. I did see it. I had a nice six-pound sea bass on my hook. Ray was on the other side of the boat, downing a beer and catching the sun's rays, so he was oblivious to what was happening on my side of the boat.

I'm trying to get my net ready to bring in my catch when I see two hands near my fish. One hand grabs the fish to steady it as the other hand pulls the hook from the fish's mouth, and then it lets it go and off swims my sea bass. I lean over the edge of the boat, and I see the most beautiful mermaid with a smile that would melt your heart. She looks up at me, laughs, and then flips over with a slap of her tail and swims away.

By this time, I'm jumping up and down like a frog on a hot griddle screaming for Ray to come and take a look. Once he finally drags his sorry ass over to my side of the boat, the mermaid is long gone. All I have to show for it is an empty hook on the end of my fishing line."

Ray: "Tell 'em how many beers you had before you saw your mermaid."

Winton: "I didn't have near enough to be seeing mermaids that weren't there. By the time she swam away, I was sober as a judge. Ain't near enough beer in the world for me to be seeing a mermaid unless there is really one there. I'll tell you this; she was the most beautiful creature I have ever seen."

Casey: "Well, the county moto…"

Everyone in the place in unison said. "Where legends live, and reality dies."

Ray: "In Winton's case, it's more like. Where legends live in Winton's beer eyes."

It took some time for the laughter to die down after that comment.

Things seemed to settle down until two girls came in and sat on the bar stools flanking Ole and me. The dark-haired one with a round face was about ten years old. The other one was a sassy-looking little redhead of about six years old.

The red-headed one started petting me. The dark-haired one looked at Ole and said. "Can I have a sip of your beer?"

Ole: "No."

Girl: "Why not?"

Ole: "You're too young. Who are you, and what are you doing in a pub? Aren't you a bit young to be in a place like this?"

Girl: "I'm Erica. That's my sister Olivia. Our dad owns this place. We always come here after school."

Olivia: "Yeah. Always. Unless we go to mom's place. She owns the Fruit and Vegetable store."

Ole: "Why don't you go to your mom's place? That seems like a better environment for two young ladies instead of a pub."

Erica: "We're supposed to go there, but mom makes us work if we are there. So we just tell dad that mom was really busy, so she sent us here instead."

Ole: "Is she really that busy?"

Olivia: "No, but our dad doesn't know that. He'll give us a soda and snacks and send us to a back table to play on our tablets to keep us busy."

Erica: "Yeah, if mom doesn't have anything for us to do, she'll send us to the back room to play on our tablets and give us a carrot or something healthy to snack on."

Olivia: "We'd rather have pretzels or chips than fruits or vegetables."

Erica: "You're new here. Who are you, and what's your dog's name?"

Ole: "I'm Ole. I just moved here from the United States."

Erica: "I've heard about you. The whole village is talking about you. You're the new Lord of the County."

Olivia: "You talk funny."

Ole: "I guess I do. You're right. I guess I am the new Lord of the County, but I prefer to just be called Ole. My companion's name is Tesse."

Olivia: "That's funny; our sister's name is Tessa; it's almost like they are related."

Olivia: "Tessa and Tesse. I can't wait to tell her the dog has almost the same name as her."

Erica: "Have you been to the castle to see the monsters?"

Ole: "I have not. I'm not even sure that there are monsters in the castle. In fact, I'm not even sure if monsters really exist."

Erica: "Of course they do. Everyone knows that. Someday Tessa and I are going to sneak up there to see them."

Olivia: "What about me? I want to come and see the monsters too."

Ole: "From what I've been told, the ruins of the castle are not very safe. They could crumble and hurt you. I think it best if you stay away from there. If there really are monsters, they might get you."

Olivia: "That's what all the grownups say."

Erica: "Weren't you ever a kid?"

Ole: "I seem to vaguely remember that I was a long time ago."

Erica: "Well, when you were a kid, and if you knew there was a castle with monsters living there, wouldn't you go to see them?"

Ole: "I probably would. However, if you do and I own the castle, you would be guilty of trespassing. I might have to sick Constable Pete on you."

Olivia: "We're not afraid of him. Are we Erica?"

Ole: "Nope, we're not. We can run faster than him. He'd never catch us."

Olivia: "If there are monster's we'll sic 'em on Pete. I bet he could beat 'em up, and while he's doing that, we'll run away."

Ole: "Well, you have some good arguments there. May I suggest you wait for a while before going there? When I have time, I'll go with you. I'd like to see for myself if there really are monsters living in the castle. Of course, you will have to get your dad's approval to go with."

Erica grabbed Ole's beer, took a quick sip, and ran off with her sister as she hollered back. "Thanks, we'll ask our dad."

I looked at Ole. "Really. You told her you'd like to see if there really are monsters at the castle. Better yet, you offered to take two little girls with you. If I remember right, Casey has another daughter named Tessa. I would be willing to bet if you take Erica and Olivia, you'll most likely get Tessa in on the bargain. I suggest we skedaddle out of her before Erica asks her dad if she and her sisters can go monster hunting with you."

Ole: "What do you mean with me? I think you mean with us."

"What makes you think I would be dumb enough to accompany you and a bunch of kids on a monster hunt?"

Ole: "You would if you weren't such a scaredy cat."

That did it. Ole knew how to push my buttons and get me worked up. One thing no dog will ever tolerate is being called a scaredy cat. "I'm in on the monster hunt," was my reply.

Erica and Olivia were impatiently waiting for their dad to finish up with a customer so they could ask about going to see monsters with Ole and me. We decided to slip out before their conversation took place.

We decided to hide out for a while just in case Casey or his girls came looking for us. We had seen the mine not far from our cottage that was located on a ledge of Longhall Mountain. It was not far from the ruins of the castles keep. Neither of us could remember a road leading to the mine, so we decided to ask for directions. A policewoman was standing on the coroner, so we approached her to ask for help.

She was in her mid-fifties, not very tall, with dark hair, a pock-marked face, and a bit on the hefty side. The name on her badge was 'Queen Bee.' We approached her and Ole politely asked if she might be able to give us some directions.

Bee: "Maybe. I guess helping people is part of my job. However, I prefer to be chasing crooks and lawbreakers. What do you want?"

She was a bit on the gruff side, and it was easy to see that being polite was not something she considered part of her job.

Ole: "We would like to visit the mine located on Longhall Mountain. Could you possibly give us directions on how to get there? We passed it by train but didn't notice any roads leading to it."

Bee: "Of course, you didn't notice any roads because there aren't any. You also didn't have to say the mine was on Longhall Mountain, for there is only one mine in the whole county, and that's where it is. The only way to get there is by train or foot. If you want to go by train, you have two choices. One is to be at the train station at eight in the morning and join the mine crew as they ride in an open ore wagon that takes them to the mine. The second option is to be at the train station at five in the afternoon when the train leaves to pick up the crew at the mine when their work shift ends.

Of course, if you take the afternoon train you'll have to make a decision. You can get to the mine and immediately return to the station with the mine workers. Or, you can stay at the mine by yourself until the train returns in the morning. If you stay, you may want to beware of the monsters. They post no guard at the mine overnight as the monsters from the castle tend to detour any would-be mine robbers.

The one other option is you can walk along the railroad tracks to the mine and come and go as you, please. It's a good hike from the village. If you walk, you will have to climb a ladder to get up to the mine. If you go by train, you can climb from the railroad wagons right onto the main mine level. It's up to you and your little dog what you want to do."

Ole: "Thank you for the information. It was very helpful."

Bee: "You're that Yank everyone is talking about, aren't you?" Lord Ole and his dog. You should really get a map of the county, then you would know where things are instead of wasting the valuable time of the village constable."

As we went back to our taxi, I commented to Ole. "Now I know why her name is Queen Bee. There is a heck of a sting to her personality."

Ole: "I heard someone at the pub say she's married to Archie."

I gave a tail-wagging smile. "Now we know why he spends most of his free time drinking and fishing."

We returned to our cottage and decided the best option for visiting the mine was to hike from our cottage along the railroad tracks. When we finally reached our destination, we looked up at the sheer rock face and saw nothing but sky. A ladder was attached to the face of the mountain, and it would be a fair climb to reach the top. Ole was game to try climbing the ladder, but the problem arose as to how to get me up there. A man climbing a ladder and trying to carry a dog under one arm was not a feasible thing to do.

Ole hollered a, "Hello. Can anyone at the mine hear me?"

An unseen voice answered. "What do you want?"

Ole: "I'd like to come up for a visit, but I have my dog with me, and I can't climb the ladder with the dog. Can you help me out?"

A face peeked over the edge of the cliff at us and could see our dilemma. "I'll send down a box for the dog, and I can pull him up. You need to climb the ladder to get here."

A wooden box was lowered on a rope, and Ole put me into it. He hollered up to have the man pull me up. Ole then began his climb up the ladder and did his best not to look down. He and Heights are not on the best of terms. As for now, he had no choice but to continue on his way up. After all, I'm the best friend he has in the whole world, so he couldn't very well abandon me at the top of a mountain, could he?

Once I saw Ole make it to the top of the ladder and put his feet firmly on the ground, I gave a tail-wagging run over to greet him. He picked me up for a few doggie kisses from me, and I got a welcoming hug and kiss on my head from him. I was just happy to see that he had made it safely up the ladder. The man that hauled me up walked over and shook Ole's hand and welcomed him to the mine.

We learned our host was the mine's owner. His name was Eastman, and this was the Eastman Mine. He was a bit over six feet tall, in his early 60s, with thinning dark hair and a welcoming smile.

Eastman: "We don't get many visitors here. The mine is not really open to the public unless by invitation. Seeing you are here, maybe I can help you."

Ole: "We got directions from one of the constables in the village. She didn't mention that the mine was not open to visitation."

Eastman: "Ah, yes. You must have talked to Queen Bee. It's no wonder she didn't mention the no-visitor policy. She's probably hoping you would come here, and I would call the police to have you escorted from the property. She lives to do things like that. Makes her feel important. There isn't much law-breaking in the village other than an occasional drunk or maybe a domestic argument so she likes to stir things up whenever she can."

Ole: "I noticed she seemed to be a bit different. By the way, my name is Ole, and this is my partner Tesse."

Eastman: "I figured you were the Yank that moved into the Poachers Rest. I can see the road leading to your place from the village. You look to be driving a sidecar rig. It's bright yellow and hard to miss even from here."

Ole: "You seem to know a lot more about me and Tesse than we know about you. We saw the mine when we first arrived here by train. You probably guessed that I'm the new owner of Longhall County, seeing that I moved into the Poachers Rest."

Eastman: "Yeah, I figured that. So I would assume you want to look the mine over. My family's held the lease on this property since the 1800s. The railway laid the tracks here to haul our ore to be processed."

Ole: "How many people do you have working for you?"

Eastman: "Six men plus myself do it all. It's hard work, and of course, we spend a lot of time underground. I mostly supervise everything from making sure the mine shafts are safe, and the timbers get replaced as needed. I also do all the paperwork and deal with the inspectors that come here to make sure everything is up to snuff. I and the men that work for me take pride in the fact we have never had a death or serious accident in the mine for over 100 years."

Ole: "That's quite an accomplishment. You should be proud of it, just out of curiosity. You said there had been no deaths or serious accidents for over 100 years. Were there some accidents or deaths before that?"

Eastman: "Unfortunately, there were a few problems in the early days. Safety sometimes took a back seat to profits. There were some cave-ins, and of course, equipment failures accounted for more than their fair share of injuries and occasionally deaths. As for my family, since we've had the mine, we take great pride in putting people over profit. With that said, you do know that our lease is good for another ten years, so I would hope you are not planning on raising our lease payment."

Ole: "To put your mind at ease I have no intention of raising anyone's leases or rents. I inherited the county from my great-grandfather, and I hope to leave everything just the way he left it when he died. I've yet to hear anyone speak badly of him or any of his arrangements, so I assume everything has been working as smoothly as can be expected, and I hope it stays that way."

Eastman: "Good to hear. I'm glad we are on the same page. Would you like a tour of the mine?"

Ole: "Yes, we would. That's actually why we came here. Just what does the mine produce? Coal, slate, or maybe lead?"

Eastman: "We happen to be one of the few places left in England that actually mines gold and silver deposits. It's not enough to be called what you Americans refer to as a bonanza, but it provides us with a comfortable living."

We walked over to the west side of the mine entrance to a heavy-duty table where a blacksmith had a forge nearby and did maintenance on tools and equipment. He also made specialty tools to handle unusual situations that popped up from time to time for which no commercial products were available to do a specific job. The blacksmith was a burly fellow, covered in grim with forearms like an oak tree. He was too busy pounding on a piece of metal to take notice of us.

Eastman pointed out a small shed made of stone that was some distance from the mine entrance. He explained that the shed held gunpowder and dynamite for use in the mine to blast sections of rock loose.

Ole was given a hard hat to wear before we entered the mine. He was also told that if I was to accompany him, it would be best if he carried me for my own safety. Rules for our tour were minimum. Watch your step as the stone floor could be slippery in places from seeping water. Watch your head, for there were some places where the rocks were jutting down from the ceiling above you. If you hear a clanking sound of wheels on steel, step aside as it means a hand car of ore is approaching or coming from behind on the rails that had been laid throughout the mine. Also, down the center of the rails was a cable that was always taught and quite easy to trip over. The cable was there to move the carts in and out of the mine via a winch system.

Luckily electric lights had been strung along the various tunnels and gave enough light to see things pretty well. Eastman told us that the bare bulb incandescent light bulbs hanging at intervals along our path were soon to be upgraded to LED lights in the near future. Much safer, more light and much more efficient, and less prone to breakage or burning out.

We passed some shafts with no lights. Eastman told us if the vein had petered out, the shaft lights would be turned off and work discontinued in that area. However, there was always a possibility that in the future, they might have to reexamine some areas as to the feasibility of continuing the search for a new vein. As for now, they had been following a fairly lucrative vein of gold for some time.

The area we were traversing slanted downward until we reached the end of the line. Two men were busy chipping away at the rock wall while a third was loading the broken rock into an ore cart.

Eastman explained that mining was still back-breaking work, and rest periods were frequent as the men needed the breaks to hydrate themselves and switch places to less strenuous jobs. Eastman picked a small nugget of gold from the floor and gave it to Ole as a souvenir of our visit.

We were then led down a shaft with the sound of running water tickling our eardrums.

Ole: "Is that the sound of water we hear?"

Eastman: "It is. It sounds like it is moving a lot faster than it really is due to the echo of the sound bouncing off the rock walls around us."

We soon came to a small river about 3 meters wide with a visibly perceptible flow of water. The area we stood in was a glistening cavern of stone with veins of quarts and even some crystals. A few stalagmites and stalactites were scattered around the cavern floor and ceiling.

Ole: "This is amazing. However, I don't understand the stalagmites and stalactites. Mines usually don't have natural caverns or crystals associated with them. As for having an underground river, wouldn't that be a valid reason to close most normal mining operations?"

Eastman: "According to most engineering theories, you would be correct in your assumptions. In fact, our mine is a bit of an anomaly defying any semblance of logic as mankind knows it. The cavern is a natural phenomenon that we feel is best kept secret from the world outside of here. As for the river being a problem, it has been a blessing as it seems to divert any excess water that might hinder our mining operation.

Ole: "Has anyone ever attempted to find the river's source or where it ends?"

Eastman: "It's source. Whoever really knows where an underground river starts? Or, for that matter, does anyone really care? Unless it's flooding their basement or their property. I guess then they would try to divert it. As for where it ends, that was fairly easy to figure out. One day we got some environmentally friendly dye and poured a bunch of it into the river. With the sea so close by, we figured that was where it would drain to. We got a rowboat and rowed along the shore by the wharf to see if we could spot the dye in the water. It took a few hours for it to show up, but it finally did. Seems the underground river empties into the sea somewhere along the bulrushes near Carol's horse stables."

Ole: "That was an interesting and novel approach to get your answer. You know this cavern is quite an anomaly for England. Caverns like this back in the States would bring in a tidy sum of money when opened to tourists."

Eastman: "There are caves open to the public in England. There's Cheddar Gorge Cave in Somerset, Hellfire Caves in High Wycombe, Chislehurst Caves in Chiskehurst, Castleton Caves in Peak District, Dan-yr-Ogof in Poweys South Wales, just to name a few.

The only thing is we are operating a working gold and silver mine that just so happens to share space with a natural cavern carved out by nature. Opening the cavern to the public would not only be a safety concern, but it would also be a high risk for theft of the gold and silver we are mining. For those very reasons, the cavern has been kept secret since it was discovered. In fact, the only ones outside of my employees who must sign a confident contract that is aware of the caverns were the owners of Longhall County, of which you are now one. So I hope that you will keep everything you see here confidential and tell no one."

Ole: "You have my word and that of Tesse's that we will tell no one."

Eastman: "The word of the owner of Longhall County and their pets has always been gospel, and so it shall continue to be so."

Ole: "Constable Queen Bee mentioned that when the last train of the day picks up the miners that, I had better be on it, or I would end up staying the night at the mine by myself. Don't you post a guard to watch over the mine at night? I would think if no one was here, it would be an open invitation for someone to try and steal gold and silver from the premises."

Eastman: "Interesting you should mention that. You will notice that Longhall Castle is at the top of the mountain and that a stone wall with steps goes from that wall to the castle. No one knows exactly when the wall was built or when the steps were added, but most certainly, it was to allow access from the Castle to the castle keep, which is located on the same ledge as the mine. Of course, that part of the story really has nothing to do with what I am about to confide in you.

I don't know if you've heard about the monsters that are supposed to be living at the castle since the 1940's or maybe it was the 1950s. The exact date doesn't really matter. It had something to do with a movie company that came here to film a movie with all the classic monsters of yore. As legend has it, the monsters took the castle over themselves to be their home away from humans. All they supposedly want is to be left alone so they can live in peace and not be bothered.

My father told me that before the monsters came to the castle, there was a night watchman at the mine. After the monsters moved into the castle, it seems that the steps from the castle to the keep started to be used by the monsters during their nocturnal wanderings. On occasion, those wanderings would lead them to check out the mine and, more directly, the river cavern, as we would later learn.

Needless to say, it became rather difficult to keep a night watchman when the likes of Dracula, Frankenstein's monster, the Wolfman, the Creature from the Black Lagoon, and others would show up at the mine. There have even been occasional sightings of Bigfoot. There were a few braver souls who worked for us as night watchmen long enough to mention that the most disconcerting creature to show up at the mine itself was some sort of gill creature. Whether it was male or female, or maybe it was both, for sometimes there were two sighted at the same time. When the watchman followed them at a safe distance so as not to be seen, he said they would make their way to the river cavern and slip into the underground river.

At first, the wild tales were ignored and blamed on the possibility of drinking on the job, or maybe it was fumes from the mine or fog playing tricks on the mind. After the sixth watchman quit and a watchman named Cory disappeared without a trace, my father decided to spend the night at the mine himself. The first two nights were uneventful, although he admitted to me that he was a bit unnerved by strange noises that seemed to emanate from the castle. He told me that he did his best to convince himself that the noises were made by the wind or wild animals.

Then on the third night, he saw a movement at the edge of the cliff where the castle is located. Being dark, he could not make out whether what he saw was an animal or a human, but it seemed to be walking upright on two legs."

"Or a monster," I whispered to Ole.

Eastman: "Somehow, my father mustered up the courage to go and investigate. He made his way to the retaining wall and slowly crept up the stairs to the castle. There was just enough moonlight for him to make out the creatures that inhabited his field of vision. You would not be amiss to think he had been drinking or hallucinating, but he swore he was cold sober, and completely in control of his senses.

He saw two figures walking side by side and talking back and forth just like you and I are talking to each other right now. The only thing is they were not human. One resembled a wolf man like you would see in a 1940s horror movie, and the other was a werewolf-like creature. Sitting on the steps of the castle were none other than the Frankenstein monster and his bride. Unlike the movie version, they seem to have reconciled and accepted each other as they were holding hands. On top of the castle's highest tower was a man in a cape who was a dead ringer for Bela Lugosi's rendition of Dracula. My father then glimpsed a mummy coming out of one of the broken walls of the castle, and he said he then thought it best be on his way before he was seen.

He ran down the stairway from the castle and high-tailed it to the ladder near the mine, which led to the railroad tracks. From there, he hoofed his way home to our family cottage.

Once word got out around the village from the night watchman and my father, it was found that it was no longer necessary to post a watchman at the mine. My father, I, and the rest of the village feel it is best to let the creatures of the night roam freely about the castle and the mine. As long as everyone leaves them alone, they have caused no trouble for any of us.

To make an appropriate end to the story. This is Longhall County where Legends live, and reality dies."

Ole: "You said that as long as the monsters kept to themselves, the people have decided to let them be. What about that Cory fellow that disappeared? Could it be possible that the monsters got him?"

Eastman: "Hard to say. He was not from Longhall County and had only been here for a short time. Most of us figure he got spooked and high-tailed it back to wherever he came from. At least that's what all of us, including the police, choose to believe."

Ole: "Seems like a rather cavalier assumption under the circumstances. With monsters roaming about the premises. Didn't the police look into it?"

Eastman: "They did. At the time, Chief Constable Jerry O'Driscol scoured the mine and the area around it as if it was a major crime scene. He kept the mine closed for a week while he conducted his investigation. He could not locate any evidence of foul play at the mine, and nobody was ever found. Seeing the mine was the place of employment. Jerry never bothered to check out the castle. He felt it best to leave that part of the mystery as it was. No use to stir up any hard feelings from those that supposedly resided there. The official police report states that the employee seemed to have left his job under unknown circumstances. That was really all the report could say. After all, it couldn't say he left due to monstrous activities."

That last statement got a laugh from all of us. We continued our tour of the mine, and its many off-shooting shafts. It was a maze of underground tunnels. In one shaft that was no longer being worked at the moment, Eastman led us to the very end of the tunnel and then flicked a switch and turned out the lights. It was very scary to be in the bowels of the earth in total darkness, with the only sound to be heard was that of dripping water and our own breathing. I, for one, was very happy when he turned the lights back on. I was almost ecstatic when we finally left the mine and came back into the light of day.

Eastman had to return to his job, and we decided to just hang out around the area so we could take the train back to the village at the end of the mine workers' shift.

With some time to kill on our hands, we decided to head to the castle keep that was on the same rock ledge as the mine. We carefully made our way around some fallen rocks and rock outcroppings until we were at the foot of the keep. In the castle's heyday, the area was probably kept clear of fallen rocks and slippery slopes, but that was no longer the case. We were now some distance from the mine, and with stories of monsters at the castle, it was doubtful that the keep had very few, if any, visitors. However, we were aware that the Ghostbusters had recently been sent to the keep and the castle to investigate strange happenings. From what we had been told, the Ghostbusters failed to fulfill their contract of investigating the area and had left in a somewhat hurried fashion.

Our approach to the keep brought us to a crumbling staircase that Ole being two-footed, had to negotiate a bit more carefully than I did. As for me having four legs and four paws on the ground, I found it to be not as challenging as I made my way quickly to the top of the steps.

To our right were the crumbled walls of what was most likely the keeps armory. Its timbered roof had long since rotted away, and its crumbled walls were all that was left to mark its long disused existence. A stairway to the battlement was still useable. We made our way up the stairs and walked carefully along the rough stones of the battlement that had moved and changed positions with age. From our vantage point, we had a good view of the village and even the sea beyond. The walls that had one time offered protection with openings for soldiers to use their bows and arrows and probably crossbows were still visible, although we were reluctant to get too close to the edges as the stone walls were cracked and crumbling in a number of places. Ole was about to walk inside the tower at the end of the battle when he noticed the floor had collapsed. He tossed a rock down the hole, and we listened for some seconds before we heard it hit the bottom. We figured that at least thirty feet separated us from falling to our deaths if we had not seen the missing floor in time.

Ole took a bunch of pictures with his cell phone, figuring this was probably the only time we would risk exploring this crumbling structure. It was part of his history, and having photos to document its present condition would not only be good for prosperity, but they may also be useful if, in the future, the structure might be worth stabilizing to keep it from deteriorating any worse than it already was. After all, England is well known for its many historical sites and ruins.

Once Ole had finished taking pictures and our exploration of this area was completed, we gingerly made our way back to the main level of the keep.

We were now at the next and final step of our exploration of the keep. Before us stood the four story high main tower. The square tower, like the rest of the keep, was showing its age. The eight windows that we could see from our vantage point were missing stones in many places giving the place the look of a horror movie haunted building. The crumbling stairs that led to a large wooden door were a bit hard to navigate even for me and my four feet. I was waiting at the top of the steps for some time before Ole worked his way up next to me. Set above the door in stone was the family crest of a shield with a hedgehog in its center, a Viking ship in two opposing corners, and a scroll signed by William the conqueror in the opposing corners. We assumed the Viking longships represented the invasion that our ancestors had repelled. The scrolls were most likely to show that the land was deeded to the Long-Hall family.

We looked at the round-topped wooden door that sat ajar in front of us. It was about six inches thick, and it took the full force of Ole's bulk to finally get its rusted hinges to give way enough for us to get it far enough open for Ole to squeeze his way inside.

Once we were inside the tower, the darkness was permeated only by the small amount of light peeking in from the open doorway and a bit of light from a crumbling window. We stood for a moment to let our eyes get accustomed to the darkness around us. There was an eerie quiet that gave Ole and me goosebumps. Maybe it was the spirits of the keeps long dead inhabitants that were spooking us.

Slowly moving about on the floor that was none to even from years of settling, Ole finally pulled out his cell phone and turned on the flashlight. He shone it along the walls revealing another room that we peeked into. It was filled with rusted armor, shields, crossbows, arrows, and clay jugs that had at one time been filled with oil that would be boiled or set on fire to rain down on attacking enemies. Ole whispered as to not disturb any lurking spirits. "This stuff would be worth a fortune on eBay."

We stepped away from the armory and made our way to a stone stairway that led to the next floor. The stair followed the circular contours of the wall as we made our way up to the next level. As we traversed the steps, small chunks of stone fell from the edges, so both Ole and I hugged the wall figuring the steps would be more stable there.

We could see that the floor on each level was constructed of eight-inch thick planks of wood. We made our way carefully along the floors to explore just in case they had rotted out and may be unsafe. Luckily they had weathered their age well, and other than a few occasional creaks and groans, the floor seemed to be stable. The upper floors were empty other than a few odd branches, leaves, and bird or bat droppings that had accumulated through the open windows over the years.

The floor of the roof's upper level had been more weather-beaten as its top was open to the elements. The rain, fog, and sun had rotted the flooring so that it had some large holes that would be easy for me to fall through and might give way under the weight of Ole's body. As we explored the open part of the tower, Ole tested each footfall with some of his weight before proceeding. Some of the areas were like sponges, having absorbed puddles of water in their uneven sections. Another rather disconcerting item was a large crack along one side of the stone walls. The crack ran from one side of the ramparts down to a full story below us. The battlement on the sides facing the mine and village had crumbled away to nothing. The battlements on the other sides were still mostly intact. We never ventured far from the stairway, as the top of the tower did not seem to be a safe area for further exploration.

The view from the top of the tower was worth our trip. On second thought, it made us both wonder if it was actually worth the risk of our lives to get to where we were.

We knew it was unlikely we would make this trip again, so Ole pulled out his cell phone and started taking pictures of not only the battlement but also of the view of the surrounding area. We had a fantastic view of Longhall Castle, Eastman mine, the mountain itself, and a great view of Hedgehoghaven Village and all the way out to the North Sea in the distance.

As we made our way back down the winding staircase, Ole made a photographic record of each room. On our way down to the second floor, a stone gave way under Ole's foot, and he slipped onto his buttocks. He managed to stabilize himself by grasping onto a protruding stone at the edge of the wall. I grabbed his pant leg in my teeth and pulled hard to keep him from going over the edge of the stairway. He and I were safe, but there was a casualty. The cell phone had slipped from Ole's hand, and we heard it hit the stone floor below us with a sickening thud. The phone's flashlight had stayed on, so it was easy for us to locate it. Ole picked the phone up, and the only real damage was a spider web crack on one corner of the screen and a long, barely visible crack that ran from the spider web to the top corner. Ole checked it over, and everything was still working.

Once we were back outside, we made our way down the outside staircase to the nice firm mountain, and we both breathed a sigh of relief.

I looked at Ole and said: "That was quite an adventure, but I think it best we don't ever do it again."

Ole: "My ass is sore from that fall on the stairs. My phone is cracked. Yet it was a great adventure. Never say never, though. Maybe someday we'll come back to chase monsters, or we might look at restoring the keep.

I just shook my head no as we made our way back to the mine. Sometimes humans don't have much common sense.

When it was time for the mine to close for the day, we joined Eastman and his crew for the train ride back to the village. Except in our case, we didn't actually go to the village. The train backed down the tracks to our cottage and dropped us off at our door. Now that's what I call service.

CHAPTER 12

As time slipped by, we became more accustomed to our new home, and hopefully, the locals became more accustomed to us 'Yanks' as they still referred to us.

We had begun to avoid spending time at Chaps Pub after school hours to keep from being badgered by Erica about when she and her sisters could visit the castle with us. It seemed that later visits after 7 pm were all right as by that time, she and her sisters had been hustled home by their mother to keep them away from the more adult patrons who were out and about.

Ole and I had done a fair amount of exploring the county by this time, although there were still a few places we hoped to check out in the near future. Of course, the castle was reluctantly on our list, even though we were more than a bit apprehensive about going there. The prospect of upsetting its inhabitants if there truly were monsters living there weighed heavy on our minds. If we did finally decide to go to the castle, we would have to keep our promise to Erica and her sisters to accompany us. One thing that could be said about Ole was that he always kept a promise. Although if Casey and Tracey became aware that we were to take the girls to the castle, that might just squash any promise we had made, and we could let the girl's parents take the blame.

One place that looked extremely interesting to visit with its promise of huge historical interest to Ole was St. Catherine's Church. However, if we decided to visit St. Catherine's and Deacon Carl happened to be there, which was a good possibility, then he would most certainly expect us to start attending Sunday services. Now Ole and I consider ourselves to be good Christians, and we are strong believers in God, the Bible and the Ten-commandments. We just happen to be a bit skeptical of organized religions. Our objection being is that when you put humans in charge of anything, they tend to lean things to their own way of thinking, which does not always coincide with what the bible says. Enough preaching from me on other things.

The fire station and clock tower were also on our visitation list, as was the empty building at the corner of the street west of Chaps pub. Those were the places that we had on today's agenda as sure spots to visit. If time permits we might squeeze in more.

The village itself was set up in a rectangular square with buildings on all four sides and an open center courtyard that contained one business building along with access to the rear of all the other buildings. Access to the center was a large opening under an archway of William's Restoration building and some walkways from Henry's Hardware store and Dr. John's Apothecary.

Our first stop was the clock tower. It was located on the far southwest corner of the village. It was made of white brick, with the roof painted red towards the top and blue at the bottom. A brass finale pointed skyward from the top of the roof. The four-faced clock was, of course, visible from all directions. We went inside and took the circular staircase to the top of the tower so we could observe the clock mechanism. When it was first built, the clock had to be wound by hand, but over the years, it had been updated to run on electricity. It was a very impressive timepiece with a history going back to the late 1800s.

Moving west to the center of the block, we crossed the street to the fire station. It was a typical small-town affair with two garage doors and a hose drying tower off to one side. An ambulance and fire truck were parked outside in readiness. A few of the firefighters were polishing the fire truck and its myriad of brass fittings to a glossy shine. As we stood watching them, one of the men stopped what he was doing and asked if we needed assistance. Ole asked if Fire Chief Dale was on duty. We were instructed to walk around to the side of the building where we would find him.

As we rounded the corner of the building, we saw two off-duty firemen playing checkers while a third man stood watching them. An old dog lay on the ground by the checker players soaking up the sun's rays.

Dale was off to the side and downwind of the checker players. He was stripping off the old finish from an antique chair, and from the strong fumes of the stripping solvent, it was easy to see why he kept downwind of anyone that was nearby. He looked over at us. "Ole, Tesse. What brings you two to the fire station?"

Ole: "Curiosity. The last time we visited a fire station was back in the States. Things there look a bit similar to here. We were sort of hoping for a tour, but we can see you're busy. Guess we didn't know firemen did furniture refinishing as well as fighting fires."

Dale laughed as he answered. "As a rule, they usually don't. We tend to have a lot of free time on our hands. You can only do so much training and maintenance of equipment. Once things are caught up, we are pretty much on our own. Of course, we can't leave the station grounds, but we can pretty much do as we please on our off times. As for me, I run an antique shop on the side. When I'm here at the station, my wife Phyllis runs the antique shop. I could use a break from refinishing this chair. The smell of furniture stripper gets to you after a while. That's why I need to work downwind from those checker players over there."

He wiped off his hands on an old rag and offered to give us a tour.

Our first stop was to check over the ambulance. It was made in the 1950s but had been kept in tip-top condition. Dale told us that two paramedics were on duty at all times. Any time the fire truck was called out, the ambulance went with it. That way, if anyone needed medical assistance or if a fireman was injured or inhaled too much smoke, the paramedics would be ready.

Next was a tour of the one and only Bedford fire truck. It was the same vintage as the ambulance and looked as if it was new. The brass fixtures on the truck and hoses glistened in the sun like gold, and the red paint of the truck shone as if it had just left the factory. Dale explained that it was built to handle any of the two-story buildings in the county. He told us that the county regulations did not allow any building over two stories high. This came out of necessity when a few years ago, Archie's three-story bakery caught fire and was a total loss as the ladder truck was only able to get to the second floor, and the flames from the fire that had consumed the third floor caused it to collapse and as it fell to the two floors below the best he and his crew could do was to keep the fire from spreading to the adjacent buildings. Luckily no one was seriously injured, although one of the firemen did suffer from smoke inhalation.

Inside the main floor of the fire station were two stalls, one for the fire truck and one for the ambulance. The floors and walls glistened with cleanliness like a hospital operating room. Off to one side was a small dispatcher's office that was manned twenty-four hours a day to take fire and medical emergency calls. A large map of the village and the surrounding county hung on the wall marking all the buildings that were in the district with notes as to any unusual locations or hazards and directions for each location.

There was another door behind the office that led to the hose drying tower. A door towards the rear of the building led to the second floor. We looked at the brass fire pole that glistened like gold that came from the second floor for a quick exit from upstairs sleeping quarters.

On the second floor were beds and lockers for the firefighters. On open hooks along one wall were firefighting coats, gloves, and helmets. Above each hook was the name of the firefighter who the items belonged to. A few of the firefighters gave us nonchalant looks as they lay in their beds reading books or taking naps.

We made our way back outside and were standing in front of the two trucks when Ole asked Dale if he had ever heard any unusual sounds coming from St. Catherine's or its attached graveyard.

Dale: "You only hear them late at night. Could be ghosts of the past or maybe a banshee. Or it might just be the wind howling past the headstones. Don't you ever tell Deacon Carl I said that he gets a bit testy about folks suggesting the church or its grounds might be haunted?"

We thanked Dale for the tour and then made our way to Olive's diner for a bite to eat. We ordered a shepherd's pie for each of us. Ole had a bottle of Squirt soda with his meal, and I had a bowl of water with mine. The place wasn't too busy, so we seated ourselves at the counter, so Olive would not have to travel about the place to serve us. Ole decided to make small talk and asked her if she knew anything about the empty corner building next to Chaps Pub.

Olive: "Years ago, it was a hotel. The best and only one in the village at that time. But when the 'Kings Head' hotel opened with larger rooms, modern plumbing, and a fancy dining room, it took most of the business away from the old place, and it was not too long after that before it fell on hard times and disrepair. For a while, there were some offices in there, but nothing that lasted very long; it was too cold and drafty, and the plumbing leaked. Now it just sits empty; most likely, the only tenants it sees nowadays are mice, rats, spiders, and a few bats. How come, you asked? You thinking about fixing the old place up and opening a business there?"

Ole: "Just curious. Tesse and I have been exploring the village, and that place caught our eye. It is such a unique stately old building. It's a shame it just sits empty, and no one is caring for it."

Olive: "We don't get much interest in opening new businesses in the village. Most folks are content with the way things are. Pretty much everything we need is right here. Rocky's tavern next door is about the only new business in the village, and it was transported from another village to here, so it's more like a very old new business. That ATV power sports shop came and went in less than a year. To modern a building for our village, that's why they demolished it. Although I guess it is still sort of going since Tony at the repair shop took over the inventory and the franchise of those CFMoto 4-wheelers, and now I hear they are even going to sell CFMoto motorcycles. Chinese stuff, so they say. If anything, they should sell Triumphs, BMW, Honda, or Piaggio Vespa wouldn't be quite so bad. German, Japanese, or Italian would be less hard to swallow than Chinese don't you think?"

Ole: "Well, the world is changing. It's a global economy nowadays, and the Chinese are doing to the world what the Japanese did in the 1960s and 1970s. Guess we just have to accept that change is inevitable.

By the way, getting back to that old building. If I wanted to take a look inside, who should I talk to about it?"

Olive: "Usually, Carol over at the bank would handle any transactions involving property in the county. Unfortunately, she seems to have disappeared, and no one knows her whereabouts at this time. I heard they hired a part-time teller at the bank, but they are not authorized to do anything other than handle the daily money transactions. I doubt they would have access to any information on the areas properties or buildings.

However, my husband, Roger, is on the bank's board of trustees. I could check with him if you wanted me to. Otherwise, if you just want to get a look inside, ask Casey over at Chaps Pub. He's next door to the place, and most of the local businesses had keys for each other in case of an emergency."

Ole: "Thanks for your help. I'll check with Casey about the key. If I have any interest in the building, I'll let Roger know."

We made our way over to Chap's pub, and Ole figured we best have a seat at the bar and order drinks to be sociable before asking any questions about the building next door. Ole made some small talk and fidgeted around a bit before broaching the subject.

Ole: "Casey, Tesse, and I have been exploring the village, and the empty building next door has piqued our interest. I was talking to Olive at her restaurant, and she thought it might be possible that you may have a key to the place. If so, and with your permission, we sure would like to see what it looks like inside."

Casey: "You know, I think I do still have the key to the place. The owner of the hotel and I each had keys to each other's places in case of an emergency. In fact, I also have a key to Kelley's arcade for the same reason, and of course, he has a key to my place. He's also my brother-in-law, so if you can't trust your relative, who can you trust."

Ole: "From a lot of folks I have met in the county, it seems most of you are related in one form or another."

Casey let out a laugh. "True enough. As for next door, normally I would send you to see Carol at the bank. She usually handles all the properties in the county that are for sale or rent. Alas, she seems to have temporally disappeared for the time being. Nice lady, it sure would be a relief for all of us to hear that she is all right. Now as for next door, under the circumstances and you being the owner of the county, I can't see any harm in letting you use my key to do a bit of exploring. If I remember correctly the power is still on in the building, but you best watch your step when you are roaming around. Could be some loose boards on the stairs going down to the basement, and I would bet that a few undesirable critters and vermin have taken up residence. Being this is England, and that is a very old building, I wouldn't be a bit surprised if a ghost or two might be lurking about."

I looked at Casey after he made the 'ghost' comment, and he didn't smile. These English folks just seem to accept as fact that ghosts are real and could inhabit a place just as well as any flesh and blood human could.

We finished our drinks as Casey went to fetch the key. He handed it over to Ole, who promised we would return it when we were done.

Standing in front of the door, Ole slipped the key into the lock. It took a bit of jiggling and effort to get it to turn. Age and corrosion had taken its toll, and a loud click finally told us that the door was unlocked. Ole pushed on the door, which had become warped over time, and with a bit of persuasion, it finally opened with a groan of hello from the rusty hinges.

We stepped inside and were greeted by the darkness and the musty smell of a building that had long been deprived of sunlight and fresh air. The windows had large moth-eaten drapes pulled over them. Ole pulled one of the drapes aside just to have it disintegrate in his hand as it came loose and crumbled to the floor, causing a puff of dust to rise into the air, even with the drape gone, the years of dirt and cobwebs on the window glass left in just enough light to see where the light switch was located. Luck was with us, and Casey was right. The switches were the old push-button style, and Ole pushed on one, which brought the large chandelier in the lobby to life. It flickered a bit, but it finally settled into a warm glow to light up the lobby. The wall fixtures followed suit with the push of a second button, and after a few minutes, my nostrils could smell the dust burning off the light bulbs as they heated up. A mouse darted across the floor, and my eyes could see its little mouse footprints on the coating of the dust of what was once a polished marble floor.

Two semi-round staircases, one on each side of the lobby, led to the upstairs. A check-in desk of carved wood with a marble top was located between the staircases along the back wall. Exploring the main floor, we found a few guest rooms which had been turned into offices that looked to have been abandoned for some time. A dining room was located behind the wall of the lobby. It had stained glass windows that lit in a rainbow of colors that splashed across the tables and chairs that had long since sat vacant of any diners. Off to the side of the dining room was the kitchen. It still had most of the everyday items either sitting or hanging from hooks that would have been used in its heyday. A few dirty dishes and some empty boxes and cans were strewn about that most likely had been left by the occupants whose offices we had seen. Of course, it made me wonder just what kind of slobs would not clean up after themselves. The last area on the main floor was the octagonal tower in one corner of the building. It had also been set up as an office and gave a nice view of the railway shops and the mountain.

Finding a door tucked away under one of the stairways, we opened it and took the stairs down to the basement. A room in the basement was locked, and its heavy wood door led us to believe something important or valuable might be behind it. Luckily there was a small arched window in the door with three iron bars running diagonally across it. Ole pulled out his cell phone flashlight and, putting his hand between the bars, lit up the room for us to see it was a well-stocked wine cellar.

The rest of the room held the remnants of a coal chute and coal bin. The coal bin was piled with old broken furniture and unclaimed pieces of luggage, which were probably kept in case the owner might someday return and ask for them. A large natural gas furnace had taken the place of the old coal-burning unit. We took that as a good sign in case we decided to occupy the building.

Making our way upstairs, we noticed that the marble steps were still in good condition with no visible chips or cracks. The ornately carved wood banisters were looking a bit weathered and dried out from use or neglect, but their strength and integrity seemed to be intact. They would be worthy candidates for a proper restoration.

The upstairs was divided into individual rooms for the guests. Most of the rooms were still furnished and looking a bit forlorn from lack of use. Looking with an eye for possible renovation Ole and I noticed that it would be possible to remove the walls of the rooms, and the upstairs could be converted into one large open area, which would fit nicely for what we had in mind if we were to occupy the building. However, we knew the village and its populace were quite conservative about change. This was, of course, brought to our attention when they forced the removal of the 'Heck of a Deal' power sports shop. We figured it would be best to do some investigating before we committed to taking over the building so we would be well prepared to face the village council.

We left the building much as we had found it. Turning off the lights and locking the door behind us, the only trace of our being there were the foot and paw prints we left on the dusty floor.

To finish our day or exploring, we decided to visit all the shops and buildings in the village's main square that had so far been neglected by us. Leaving the key at Chaps, we walked past the building we had just explored and rounded the corner to head south. The first building we came to was Lovett's Lamb and Meats. We entered and took in the pleasing aroma of curing and smoked meats. The owner Ray was at the counter and offered us a sample of some of his custom-made sausage and jerky. We strolled around and checked out the many offerings in the glass showcases. As we left, Ole told Ray we would certainly be back at a later date to make some purchases.

Next, we bypassed Winton's 'In Cod we Trust' restaurant as we had already visited that establishment.

The post office was a quick visit as there was not much to see. It was, well, just a post office. Lates was out on his rounds delivering the mail. While he was gone, a sign at the counter read that he would be back at 3pm.

At the 'Kings Head' hotel, we met the proprietor Nikki who, after a brief visit, we learned she was married to Henry of 'Henry's Hardware and General Store'. She gave us a brief tour of the hotel with its small dining area and nicely equipped rooms, and we were soon on our way.

At the Penny & Pound Bank, we met the temporary cashier Caraline who was in charge during Carol's absence. She told us her mother, Valerie owned Natural Healing Massage, and her father owned Centimental Coin-ops. We were beginning to believe this was a very family-oriented village.

The hobby shop was next, and we were greeted by Oscar, who ran the place along with his part-time job of helping out his father, Henry, at the Hardware store. Oscar let us brose to our or should I say Ole's heart's content. He was enamored by the large selection of 00 scale model trains, of which Hornby models seemed to dominate the selection.

Rounding the corner as we bypassed Henry's Hardware store, we came to Williams Yard Repairs and Restorations, owned and operated by fire chief Dale on his days off from the fire department. Dale was across the street, so we wandered back to the fire station to pump him for some information about the restoration business. We told him in strict confidentiality that we might be interested in having some work done to a building we were considering occupying. Dale told us he could handle any wood refinishing from furniture, counters, cabinets, and banisters. What he could not do himself, he would turn over to John, his jack of all trades, who could do most everything else from remodeling, plumbing, electrical, and most anything else that might pop up. Ole thanked him and said we would most likely be in touch.

The Hardware store and the Williams building took up this short block, so we rounded the corner to 'Ye Olde Tea Shoppe', which is run by Casey and Tracey's daughter Tesse when she was not attending school. Ole and I have not yet become 'English' enough to be tea drinkers. How utterly un-English of us. We found she did have hot cocoa on her menu, so that's what we ordered. There were two older ladies sitting at one of the tables discussing their children who had grown and no longer had time for their poor old mothers. Tessa came and sat at our table as she knew us from Chaps pub. She told us the history of her shop and how it had been in this location for over two-hundred years. She was the perfect hostess, and we had a very pleasant time visiting with her. Well, that is until we were leaving. She whispered to us so that the two ladies would not hear. "Erica says you are going to take us to the castle. I hope it will be soon."

The next stop was Dingmann's Clothier for Men and Women and Mortuary. Even though both businesses occupied the same building, they were discretely separated by a wall and had separate entrances. We had met Doug, the owner at Chaps Pub, and when he saw us come in, he turned over the customer he was waiting on to one of his clerks even though Ole told him we were just browsing and didn't need any assistance. Doug insisted we take a tour of his shop, and like a typical salesperson, he made sure to show us a wide selection of shirts, pants, suits, shoes, ties, stockings, and even undergarments. He explained that everything in his shop was top quality, and he had a tailor and a seamstress who could custom-make anything for the discerning customer who wanted a one-of-a-kind garment.

Over Ole's polite refusal to purchase anything, our tour took us to a rear door of the dividing wall to the mortuary. We were given a grand tour of the embalming room and the preparation area. We then entered a showroom for the caskets. We were suddenly shocked when a person sat up from inside one of the caskets to greet us. It seems Pierce was laying in the casket he had picked out for himself for when his day on earth ended.

Pierce: "You know you can never be too prepared. I figure if I am to rest eternally in this casket, it should be comfortable. Plenty of shoulder room, and I had Doug add a bit of extra padding to the mattress, and I brought one of my own pillows from home. I do believe I will happily spend eternity in here."

Doug just shrugged it off and led us to a small chapel that was used for those who had no particular religious affiliation. We were glad when the tour had ended, and we left the mortuary and enjoyed the sunshine and fresh air. I, for one, found the mortuary to be a bit morbid and smelling of formaldehyde and death.

We walked past the next building, which was empty and had a large sign plastered across its front, 'Shop for Sale.'

Next up was another of our Chaps acquaintances. Dr. John's Dentist, Doctor, Medicine, and Apothecary. A large tooth protruded from the front of the building, and a row of large teeth was visible along the edge of the roof. Apothecary bottles lined the front window. A bell chimed as we entered the front door. The receptionist asked what we needed. We said we just came in to look around as we were visiting all the local businesses. John must have recognized Ole's voice and came from the side room to greet us. He had a patient in his dental chair but explained that he was waiting for a crown to set up and he had time to give us a brief town. As we were about to leave, he said, "Remember if you need any medical or dental care, just give me a call any time, day or night."

A place called Olson's Slot Shoppe had a closed sign on the door, and the lights were off. We could make out what looked to be a collection of eclectic items for sale through the front window.

Next door to the shop was another building that was empty and had a for rent sign on the door. I mentioned to Ole that if we decided to go ahead with our plans for the old hotel building, this might make a nice gift shop to run in conjecture with our other business.

We made our way into Natural Healing Massage and met the owner Valerie, who said we could just call her Val. Seeing we were new in the village, she offered Ole a free massage. Unfortunately, she did not offer one to me; darn humans get so much free stuff compared to us dogs. He, of course, accepted, and he was fine with the arrangement until he had to strip down to his skivvies. However, it was not quite as embarrassing for him as she told him to cover up with a sheet as she waited in the other room to be discreet. I was allowed to stay and watch. I must say that I had a few good tail-wagging smiles as Ole's back and sore legs got a workover that brought tears to his eyes. The two of them carried on with some small talk in between the cartoonish nasty words that Ole mumbled when Val hit the really bad stiff muscles which seemed to dominate much of Ole's body. Their conversation told us that Val was the sister to Nikki and Casey. She was also the mother of Caraline, Victoria, and Kaylynn as well as the wife of Kelley. In fact, if you took all the relatives she was related to in the village, they made up a good portion of the local inhabitants. Once the massage was over and Ole got dressed, he did have to admit he felt better, and he actually made an appointment to see her again in a month.

Next in line was Tracey's Fruit and Vegetable shop. We had seen Tracey at Chaps Pub, so we recognized her. She was Casey's wife, and that made her Val's sister-in-law. She gave us a quick tour of her little shop which didn't take very long as it was set up like a typical little grocery store which was, of course, dominated by fruits and vegetables. After a pleasant little visit, she sent us on our way with a bag of grapes as a gift.

Ole and I were both excited about our next stop. Archie's Bakery. A fancy wood sign in the shape of a baker holding a chalkboard stood outside the shop and advertised the daily specials, which were pecan pies and date-filled cookies. Of course, that brought a smile to Ole's face and a tail wag from me. Both of those are our favorites. There was no doubt we would be making a purchase here.

Archie gave us a welcoming greeting and a hardy handshake as we recognized him from where else but Chaps Pub. I remember he had false teeth, and with all the surgery delights in his establishment, it was no wonder he had lost all his teeth to testing and eating his product line. A bit of a paunch on his tummy confirmed he was a connoisseur of his own stock of goods. Ole and Archie hit it off well and had a jovial discussion about all their favorite pastries. Ole left Archie with an order for three pecan pies and two-dozen date filled cookies which we would pick up later. I mentioned to Ole that were a lot of sweet treats to have around the cottage, and it would be awfully tempting for us to eat them in a binge of ecstasy. Ole justified the purchase by saying we could freeze most of them for a later date.

We walked slowly by the Hedgehoghaven Theater, which was built in the Art Deco style so prevalent in the 1930s. The marquee advertised 'The Rise of Gru.' Ole and I agreed we would add seeing it to our to-do list. As we made our way past the theater, we almost bumped into a tramp with a bowler hat on his head, a small mustache, and twirling a cane. If we didn't know better, we could have sworn it was Charlie Chaplin. Then again, this is Hedgehoghaven 'where legends live, and reality dies.'

The next building was a small brick structure that was sandwiched between the large buildings that flanked it; the entrance was inset on one corner near the theater. An enclosed protruding window box dominated the second floor. A large 'for rent' sign let us know that it was looking for a tenant.

As far as Ole was concerned, we saved what we believed to be the best till last. Ole loves museums, bookstores, and hobby shops, but his true passion is reserved for old coin-operated amusements and arcades. This place looked to be the king of arcade buildings. It was a large two-story tall brick building with a corner entry. Its name was wrapped around both sides in large letters, 'Centimental Coin-ops.' Above the door, it stated 'Kelley coinopoligist.' Various coin-operated machines lined the outside walls of the building as they sat on the sidewalk beckoning for the loose change of any passersby. There was Ms Pacman, some Allwin penny slot machines, a Wizard Clock, penny scale, Wurlitzer jukebox, and even a strength tester. This was the only building on the block that had a crowd of people around it. From teenagers to adults, and to our surprise, we were pretty sure that Scooby-Doo and Shaggy, the South Park kids, the Simpson Family, and of course, Mario, Luigi, and the Princess were all part of those lingering about.

Making our way through the crowd, we finally got inside the building. Assorted games from past to present greeted us with sights and sounds from video games, pinball machines, fortune tellers, flipping balls of Allwin slot machines, the clank of handles and reels spinning on vintage slot machines, and the whir and talking sounds of new slot machines with their ticket in ticket out mechanisms. It was quite evident that gambling was legal in Longhall County.

As we stood in amazement, we were approached and greeted by Kelley, the owner. A bit taller than Ole with a bald head, glasses, and a bit of a belly paunch, he had the air of a game-loving geek. He was very friendly, and having met us before at Chaps Pub, he quickly dismissed with any formalities and offered to show us around. It was a trip of nostalgia from modern games to games and amusements from the turn of the century. The back room was filled with old games waiting to be restored. We found out that Kelley, his wife Val, and their three children lived upstairs. After the tour ended, Kelley gave Ole a handful of tokens and told us to enjoy ourselves. Ole thanked him and told him of our day's adventure of visiting the local businesses and how, as a special treat, we had saved his establishment for last. Kelley quickly informed us that we had missed one. It was a shop hidden from the mainstream business area, which actually made the owner happy as he liked to be a bit under the radar, so to speak. The shop was located in the center of the block behind all the other buildings. The best way to access it by vehicle was through the archway at Williams Restorations or by a few discreet entrances between some of the main street businesses. Kelley told us the quickest way to get there from his place was through the back door, which he guided us to from what we had thought was the last commercial business of our day's adventure.

Once we were behind Kelley's, the shop we were looking for was very visible. It was a two-story high white stucco building. Large black letters on the building announced the name 'Kilroy's Slot Machines.' A large drawing of the Word War Two Kilroy figure took up most of the building's front wall. However, what really caught our attention was a huge green Kilroy figure peeking over the peak of the tiled roof.

We walked through the door, and as we entered the store, it took Ole's breath away. Wall-to-wall displays of slot machines quickly overloaded my poor Ole's senses. He had not seen such a sight since his days of doing the Chicagoland Antique Slot Machine and Advertising show in St. Charles, Illinois. With his heart beating like a drum, he started to make his way along the maze of machines. Of course, there was a large selection of English machines with many versions of Allwins; there were also imports from Mills, Jennings, Watling, Pace, Rockola, Sega, Aristocrat, and Automat, almost all of which were set up to use the old large English penny. One very unusual machine made by BDR of England resembled a stainless steel bread box, or is that bread bin? There were a number of newer machines and even one that had a Monopoly game theme. The crown of the collection seemed to be a 1906 Mills upright roulette-style machine called a Dewey. Its Oak cabinet with fancy trim dripped with history.

It did not take long before we were approached by Kilroy himself. He was just a tad taller than Ole, and the two of them looked to be close to the same age. The two of them immediately hit it off. Ole had a fair size collection of slot machines and arcade games, which he had left behind in Minnesota. Of all the places we had been to since coming to England, this was the one place that Ole felt very much at home. There was no need to feel out of place for him as he and Kilroy spoke the same language, a language foreign to most, the language of antique slot machines. I knew it would be some time before Ole was ready to leave, so I found a comfortable spot off in a corner and curled up to take a nap.

CHAPTER 13

As I had expected, the visit to Kilroy's lasted late into the evening. We did not arrive back at our cottage until after midnight. I was sniffing out a good area to do my before-bed duties when something quickly brushed past my paw.

My eyes noticed a spiny-looking little eight-inch-long critter cowering between two rocks along the wall of the cottage. It rolled into a ball with its spines pointing outward as I cautiously approached. I softly said, "no need to be afraid. I won't hurt you. I have never seen a creature like you before. I assume you are a hedgehog for which the village is named. My name is Tesse. I'm a Shih-Tzu dog, and my human Ole and I live in this cottage. We recently moved here from the United States."

It took a bit, but the hedgehog slowly uncurled, and his snoot twitched as he took in my scent. Meekly he said, "my name is Current. I live here with my family. We don't mean any harm to your property. We mostly live on berries and insects. Lord Long, who lived here before with his family and servants, let us be. Can we expect the same from you and your master?"

I told him he could. With that said, he bid me farewell and scurried off into the bushes.

I went back inside the cottage and told Ole about my meeting with Current the hedgehog. Although he was busy on the computer, he said it was a shame he didn't get to meet him. Then he continued his search for information on St. Catherine's Church, figuring it would be an interesting place for us to check out on our next trip to the village.

Ole: "Would you like me to tell you a bit about St. Catherine's history?'

Of course, I knew that even if I said no, Ole would tell me anyways. So, I said the only thing I could say. "Sure, I'd love to hear all about it."

Ole: "St. Catherine's church was built in the 12th century as a chapel of Ease because it was more than 5 miles away from the nearest parish church. The church was built on land commissioned by William the Conqueror on Christmas day, 1085. It was built by the Long family on land that was given to them by William the Conqueror for the many deeds of valor they had performed in past battles.

St. Catherine's was built in the Norman Romanesque style of architecture, which was very popular after the success of the conquest in 1066. It was held by the diocese of Guildford until it was given to the Black Friars {Dominicans} in 1338, with the Dominican Sisters having a presence in Hedgehoghaven until 1348. The church was held by the Dominicans until 1538 when King Henry VIII imposed the dissolution of Monasteries. The Dominicans were seen as too powerful and authoritarian in England at this time since the trial of Queen Catherine was at the Black Friar in Longdong in 1529. When the remaining Dominicans fled to Belgium, the church was reclaimed by the diocese of Gilford and served by the Anglican Church until 1850, when the laws were relaxed, and the population around the land became more Roman Catholic.

St. Catherine's church was re-consecrated by the Bishop in 1851 and was served by the diocese of Guildford until it was offered back to the Black Friars in 1938.

Pretty interesting, huh?"

All I could say after that long, drawn out, boring narrative of historical facts was. "Sure, I can't wait to visit it."

My 'can't wait' comment did not take long to come to fruition. We soon left our cozy little cottage and made our way outside to be greeted by an overcast sky with fog so thick it made my fur damp. We boarded our three-wheel taxi and headed off in the direction of the village. We parked in an open spot at the far end of Rocky's Tavern so as not to fill up a space for any of his potential customers. Rocky's didn't open until noon, and it still being early morning, we figured he wouldn't mind. Depending on how long we hung out at the church, we figured we might just pop into his place for an afternoon nip. I, for one, was hoping we would be long gone from St. Catherine's before Rocky's opened. Not that I wouldn't mind a bit of a nip, I just preferred not to hang out at an age-old church or even a newer church for any longer than necessary.

Standing next to our Norwegian taxi, we had a good view of St. Catherine's. Ole, ever the amateur historian, pulled a sheet of paper from his back pocket. "Tesse, I've got a printout of some of the details of the church. Would you like me to read them to you?"

Being raised by Ole to be polite, I said, 'sure, I'd love to hear all about it."

Ole: "The long narrow St. Catherine's building is three stories high and made of limestone bricks built in the Norman Romanesque style. The roof consists of slate shingles with a 4.5-meter bell tower built onto the front."

I felt a need to at least let Ole know I was paying attention. "Wait just a minute, partner. Remember, we're from America. Just how tall is 4.5 meters?"

Ole: "Sorry about that. Let me google it. Ok, it's about 14 feet 9 inches. The bell tower is also made of limestone bricks with some volcanic rocks spaced randomly throughout for aesthetics. The doors are situated at ground level, with paving stones in front of them to form a small patio. The front arched doors are made of imposing solid oak standing 3 meters high at the peak, and yes, before you ask, that would be roughly 9 feet 10 inches. The door is 15 centimeters thick or about 6 inches. The door is a light gray color, as if it had been painted white at some point in time but had faded darker with age and the elements. Two large hinges, one towards the top and one near the bottom, are black in color and stretched out to the total width of the doors. Both hinges are shaped like decorative old church keys. The door is recessed into the wall by way of a large decorative arch and pillars which are carved into the limestone."

Carl had noticed us from the graveyard where he had been tending to some of the graves. He quickly approached us as if he expected us to flee in terror. I must admit that it did cross both of our minds. Carl shook Ole's hand and patted my head as he welcomed us to St. Catherine's, offering us a guided tour. Which Ole decided for both of us might prove interesting. I think we both knew that Carl's offer was not so much an invitation but an expectation that we would accept.

The old black hinges made a high-pitched squeal in protest to the damp English weather as Carl opened the doors to invite us in. The few penitents in the church turned in disruption to see Deacon Carl leading a stranger and his dog into the vestibule.

The vestibule was basically a small porch where the church bulletins were posted on a 46x46 cm piece of cork board as well as any news or information about the goings on in Hedgehoghaven Village or Longhall County.

On the opposing right side of the vestibule was posted a document of the blessing of the church with a picture of Pope Pius XI dated 1938 acknowledging the return of the Dominicans.

Before we entered the main body of the church, Deacon Carl whispered to Ole that we were about to enter into a house of God and that it would be wise to keep our voices lowered out of respect for the sacred space and the people that were currently there praying.

From the vestibule, Carl led us into the Narthex, which was located at this point under the choir loft at the back of the church. The Narthex ran the entire width of the church and extended six meters [19 feet, 8 inches} into the Nave, allowing room for the choir. The choir loft was supported by four large oak beams set equally at three meters {9 feet, 10 inches} apart. Two small wood columns about 1 meter {3 feet, 4 inches} tall and painted white standing on each side of the entry door. A large statue of Mary holding the child Jesus was centered on the back wall. On the left of the north wall was a small stand of votive candles in red glass holders placed in front of the statue.

On the right or south side of the church was a large statue of St. Dominic. This statue stood on a recessed shelf built into the back wall and was about 1 ½ meters {4 feet, 11 inches} tall. It depicted a simple, humble man wearing a white Alb cloaked with a black hood and cape. The statue held a 40-centimeter {1 foot, 4 inches} branch of white blooming flowers in his right hand, which was positioned across his chest. His left had held an open book so that a passerby could read it. Across the book's open pages, written in large bold letters, was the Latin word 'VERITAS', which translated to English is 'Truth'.

As we walked forward into the 'Nave," or main body of the church, Deacon Carl pointed out the Arcades situated on both sides of the church, paroling the aisles. The term 'arcade' being inside of a church, of course, piqued both Ole's and my interest.

Ole: "Arcade, huh? Video Bible trivia, perhaps. Bingo, for sure. Maybe even a shooting gallery, you know, the sound of guns going pew, pew, pew from the pews!"

I, of course, thought it was tail-wagging funny. Deacon Carl did his best to hold back his laughter, but a few chuckles and a smile escaped from him at Ole's religiously inept sense of humor.

Carl quickly brushed aside Ole's attempt at humor and got back down to the serious business of the church's construction. "Of course, we do have some 'pews' in the church but no games or shooting galleries. This arcade is a part of the structure. Unlike a colonnade which are columns that hold up a flat beam, an arcade has columns that support arches that help to hold up the ceiling. On both sides of the church, you will notice there are four large columns with arches between them that support the ceiling."

The ceiling was painted light blue which moved to a darker shade of blue as it went towards the center. Stars were painted along the perimeter, and in the center was a painting of Jesus. He was holding a cross in his left hand and signaling a blessing with his right hand using his thumb, index, and middle fingers. He was depicted riding on a cloud with two small cherubs on the bottom of the cloud holding him up.

I had to admit it was a very impressive scene as I stood below looking up at it.

Hanging on the walls running up and down the aisles were paintings of Jesus depicting various stages of his crucifixion. The paintings were 45 x 60 centimeters {1 foot, 6 inches by 2 feet} with simple wooden frames incorporating a small cross at the top center. Under the paintings were small glass candle holders. According to Deacon Carl, these paintings are visuals used in prayer known as the 'Stations of the Cross' where the penitent follows Jesus in the biblical telling of his passion calling to him that he is also a disciple of Jesus ordered to take up his own cross and follow him. The stations were numbered 1-14, starting from the left side front of the sanctuary running down the rear of the Nave, and coming forward on the opposing side ending at the last station near the front.

The floor of the church was made of gray tile in the area of the pews, and the center aisle was made of white and gray marble, which proceeded up the main aisle to the cheval arch, after which the sanctuary's floor was covered in red carpet. There were twelve rows of pews on each side of the main aisle, each being about 2 meters [6 feet, 7 inches] across, with each row seating six people. On each side of the pews were narrower aisles about 1 meter {3 feet, 4 inches} across.

Carl: "Here's an interesting tidbit of information that I bet you don't know. Pews are a relatively recent development within the architecture of churches. For over a thousand years, people would come to church and stand or kneel throughout the service. It wasn't until the 14th century when stone benches were placed for the elderly at the side of the church, and then in the 15th century wooden benches were introduced."

I'm not sure how old Deacon Carl is, but I, for one, do not think that the 14th or 15th century introduction of pews would be considered a more 'recent' introduction of sitting down in church.

At the front of the church, opening as if a doorway to another world, stood the chancel arch. This magnificent monument was intricately carved into the limestone wall separating the nave and the shorter room containing the sanctuary space. Pillars were carved into both sides, and an array of oak and maple leaves carved into the stone formed the upper arch as if it were a forest canopy. Just above the caved pillars running across the arch was a large oak beam. The beam had a crucifix at the top center and carvings of John on the left and Mary on the right. Along the top were carved tulips.

Carl: "This wood beam is what is left of the old Rood Screen. The Screen itself dates back to the late 14th century. It was a very ornately carved wooden cell wall that separated the secular people in the Nave from the religious in the sanctuary. While the Rood Screens are still used in Greek Orthodox and Anglican churches, they were removed from Roman Catholic churches in the year 1563 at the Council of Trent. The Bishops decided that the Rood Screen blocked too much of the view of the altar. Because of its beautiful artwork and its history, the parish decided to leave the top of the screen in place."

On the left side of the Chancel arch stood the pulpit. Protruding from the wall on top of four steps making a small staircase stood a dark brown stained balcony made of wood paneling which looked as if it was made to fit at most one person. The paneling opened on the right side to make a small passage that wrapped around the back and up the wall about 2.4 meters {8 feet} from its base and jutted out from the wall to form a canopy. The canopy curved back down towards the front of the pulpit. Hanging from the bottom rim of the canopy was a 1.5 meter {4 feet 11 inches} opening adorned with six wood tassels.

Carl: "The original pulpit was made of stone and built about the same time as the church, but age and use took its toll. So, in the mid 1500s, the current one was installed to replace it. This particular pulpit came from a church that was renovated in southern Germany and is made of Linwood. William of Ockham is said to have given a speech here in 1321 in which he gave his teaching of implicitly understanding and defining items of faith and science. Unfortunately, the sermon was too complicated for most of the village folk to understand."

On the right side of the Chancel Arch was an ancient-looking six-sided font. Honed from a single block of limestone and standing about 1.2 meters {4 feet} tall with a large bowl carved into it to hold water. Each side of the water basin has flowers with six petals carved on them.

Carl: "This is our baptismal font. It is original to the church and dates back to the late 12th century. Originally it stood at the back of the church, right at the beginning of the pews. It was moved to the front of the church in the 1960s when more baptisms were being held during the masses instead of being done separately."

Looking past the Chancel arch was the sanctuary. It was in a smaller room with an arched timber ceiling the same height as the peak of the Chancel arch. It had limestone walls with a tri-window at the back wall depicting Jesus 'Agony in the Garden' with an inquisitive-looking Jesus at the center with Peter asleep on a rock and at his left, John laying down asleep against a tree on his right.

Two more windows graced the side walls, one on each side with a depiction of Saint Michael, the archangel holding a spear and standing triumphantly on the devil. On the left was Saint Gabriel, the archangel holding a branch of lilies in his left hand and raising his right hand in declaration of right.

The entire sanctuary was raised one step higher than the rest of the Nave and contained two pews on each side facing each other in the monastic choir 'this is where the nuns sat' and two alters, one Low and one High. The Low altar was two meters {6 feet 7 inches} long, one meter {3 feet, 4 inches} wide and 1 ½ meters {4 feet, 11 inches} high. It was made of oak with a carved inlay on the front depicting the Last Supper. Draped over the top of the altar was a green linen cloth with gold crosses along its border. White beeswax candles sat at each top corner.

The High Alter was made of ornately carved oak and was four meters {13 feet, 1 inch} long, 1 meter {3 feet, 4 inches} wide, and 1 ½ meters {4 feet, 11 inches} high with a carved wooden backdrop behind it. The backdrop was 1 meter {3 feet, 4 inches} tall with carvings depicting various angels and saints.

At the center back of the altar was a gold-plated box 'tabernacle' with a lockable cross printed on the door. On top of this box was a small thirty centimeter {12 inches} crucifix. This alter was also draped in a green linen cloth with gold embroidery around the edges. Standing on both sides of the gold box were three pointed candelabras that held candles in ascending and descending order. Both candelabras were positioned so that their highest candle was nearest the box and the lowest candle was furthest away. On the right side of the High Alter was a 1 meter {3 feet, 4 inches} tall Roman style scroll top pillar holding a staff with a lantern hanging from its top. The lantern contained a candle in a red glass holder.

Carl: "The red candle is considered the Sanctuary lamp. When it is lit it signifies the presence of the consecrated elements within the Tabernacle. When the faithful pray before the Tabernacle, they are reminded that Jesus is truly present here and to contemplate the mystery of him becoming a man."

In front of the main altar was a noticeable dip in the floor. Almost as if a small section was sinking. Of course, I pointed this out to Ole and told him he should ask Carl about it.

Carl: "I'm glad you asked about that. Legend has it that back in the 15th century, there was a prideful Laird of the land who came to power after his father's passing. He had become jealous of the Priest always having a large host. Thinking that he had the most power in the land, he thought he should be given the largest piece. One Sunday at mass, right before communion, the Laird came forward and took the large host right out of the Priest's hands. Immediately the stone beneath his feet turned into quicksand, and a supreme pressure came over him, and the Laird started to sink. Realizing the dire nature of his situation, the Laird cried out for the Priest to help him. He cried out, 'Forgive me, Father. Consume this host before the ground consumes me!' the Priest took the host from the Laird's hands, and, eating it, the Laird was set free. Of course, from that time on, the Laird had a renewed focus on life. The dip in the floor was from the quicksand and should be a reminder for us all to live simple lives.

However, some of the villagers contribute the sinking of the floor to another legend. It concerns a former pastor of the church a, Father Thomas Thayer. He was a rotund man with an affinity for fish and chips. According to rumors he was 2 meters {6 feet, 7 inches} tall and almost twice as round. He was the kind of man in which, when the Cardinal and Bishop would visit parishioners he, would genuflect and say 'hello you're Grace' to the Bishop and kneel and say 'hello your Eminence' to the Cardinal. Then Father Thayer would show up, and the villagers, in jest, would say, 'oh, my God.' The Father's saintliness was also a legend in the area. It was said that one year he and his companions were on a pilgrimage to a nearby shrine and that they came upon the site of a bridge that had been washed out due to that year's flooding. It is said that, like Moses and the Red Sea Father Thayer divided the river in two by wading into its waters, allowing him and his companions to continue on their journey. Some of the villagers claim that an emancipated wind that day may have caused the waters to temporarily divide."

Ok, something was not quite right with the second story. I looked at Ole and asked what Father Thayer had to do with the sinking floor of the church. Ole looked at me and shrugged his shoulders. I guess it was a conundrum best left alone.

Carl: "Ole, if you and Tesse would like to follow me to the back of the church, I can show you where I get ready for mass."

Carl led us to a door at the north side of the aisle. The room we entered was very small. Approximately 3 meters by 3 meters {9 feet, 10 inches by 9 feet, ten inches} square yet as tall as the main church. The walls were made of sandstone blocks, and there were arches built into the wall with thin sandstone plates stacked beside each other to make the curve of the arch. Along the wall were plain solid maple lockers and cabinets that contained the white Albs plus the red, green, white, purple, rose, and black chasubles that the Deacon and the Priest wear.

What really caught the eyes of Ole and me was a malicious-looking door that was set into the back wall between the lockers. The door was cut about 1 meter {3 feet, 4 inches} into the stone wall, almost as if it had been done as an afterthought. It looked to be heavily made, much like the front door of the church. It was probably black at one time but had faded to an ominous gray over the years. Unlike the front door of the church, which had hinges shaped like church keys, this door had devilish-looking hinges that looked like three-pronged pitchforks.

What actually drew our attention to the strange-looking door was that both Ole and I could hear a faint eerie sounding noise. It sounded like metal chains scrapping over metal pipes, almost like moaning, or maybe it was just our imagination, or it might just be hissing steam escaping from a leaky boiler.

Ole: "Can I ask where that door leads to?"

Carl: "It leads down the steps to the old crypts beneath the church. They have been locked up and neglected for years. A wall separates that area from the boiler nowadays."

Ole: "Sounds like some strange noises coming from there. Haunted, maybe?"

Carl: "Don't be silly. Probably just the boiler. Our heating system is very old and needs replacing."

Ole: "Maybe we should go down and investigate. I know a bit about boilers. We used to have one in the dairy milk bottling business that we used for generating steam for bottle washing and heating. You sure wouldn't want to take a chance that it might explode and destroy the church or maybe injure or kill some of your parishioners."

Carl: "I really don't know much about boilers, but I'm sure by the grace of God it will be just fine. Besides, I really do need to get going. I have an appointment that I cannot be late for."

Ole: "I understand. If you don't mind, Tesse and I can go down and take a look at it. You can be on your way; I promise we will be quick about it. Better safe than sorry. You know, if it's not the boiler, we might just think you have someone chained up down there. You do know there is rumor's in the village that something strange has been heard from the church late at night. Old wives gossip, for sure. Just teasing you, is all. Hope you don't take offense. We'd love to check out the boiler, just for safety."

Carl: "Silly villagers and their rumors, like you said, just gossiping old ladies and the drunkards at the pubs are no better. Just to dispel any more rumors, I will take you down there myself for a quick look around. I am quite sure you will not find any nefarious happenings. We do need to make this quick as I really do have other things I need to attend to."

For someone who had just been so meticulous about showing us the church and going into such detail, it did seem rather strange to Ole and me that all of a sudden, Deacon Carl's tone had changed, and he seemed to be so reluctant about showing us the underground chamber of St. Catherine's.

Carl reluctantly pulled an old cast iron key from a hidden pocket inside of his jacket and unlocked the door leading to the crypt, or, as he liked to call it, the boiler room. He lit a candle whose flickering light would be our guide down to the lower level. As the door opened, there was a rush of cold air, and the putrid smell of fermentation filled our nostrils. As I let out a sneeze, my first thought was that we might be entering an old crypt filled with dead bodies. My second thought was that I hoped we would not be joining them in their eternal rest or eternal torment, as the case may be.

Carl led the way as we moved through the door, and we followed him with increased trepidation as to what may be waiting for us down below. A boiler or restless spirits? That was the question. Ole whispered to me this might just be Dante's Inferno, and the motto 'abandon all hope ye who enter here' might be appropriate.

The three of us carefully made our way down the 180-degree circular staircase with only the candlelight to guide us. Once we reached the bottom of the staircase, Carl's hand fumbled along the wall, searching for the light switch. "Aw, here it is." He said as he flicked on the switch. Five old early-era Edison light bulbs flickered a moment before they settled into a warm yellow glow. We were standing in a room shaped much like an old cavern carved from bedrock and well below the church above us. Carl mentioned that the lights had been installed well before his time, and he really had no idea how long it had been since this area had been electrified.

I whispered to Ole. "A bit creepy, isn't it?"

Ole: "No more so than Doctor Frankenstein's laboratory."

Scattered around were old wood crates, boxes, a few discarded statues of angels and saints, a broken Christmas manger scene, and weird carvings and words on the walls and the ceiling. The carvings and the words were of whirling vortexes and strange creatures, some of which resembled gargoyles from the tops of medieval buildings. On the far side of the room was a large oak door with a symbol on it. The symbol looked to be a plus sign inside a circle and had been recently painted with white paint that contrasted with the aged brown color of the door.

Ole: "That painting on the door over there seems to look almost a bit satanic. I realize that in the past, sometimes ancient religions incorporated some of their past symbols as they accepted Christianity. That symbol looks like it might have such a past, as do some of the symbols on the walls and ceiling. By the way, what's behind the door?"

Carl: "That room leads to the crypts. It's sacred. For someone like you, it would be just a bunch of old bones from the past. The boiler is in this room over here if you want to take a look at it."

We made our way through an open arched door into the boiler room. The boiler was ancient, and the walls were covered in asbestos which at one time was the thing to do. Streams of rusted red water leaked from some of the seams, and puddles of rusty water were evident throughout the room. A few of the stave bolts had either rusted through or popped off from pressure, and steam slowly wafted its way towards the ceiling, which was evident by the asbestos cloth hanging down from dampness. The pressure gauge glass was cracked, and the arrow lay forlornly at the bottom of the gauge, having rusted and fallen off for who knows how long ago. Ole tried to turn the safety valve lever, but it was rusted solid and wouldn't move. The coal chute that came from behind the church was filled with dirt and dust, not a good combination to shovel in with the coal to stoke the boiler.

Ole: "Can I ask who maintains the boiler?"

Carl: "Mostly me. But as you can see, it needs some work. The church can't afford to have a regular maintenance man."

Carl was cut off abruptly by a high-pitched screech and the sounds of chains clanging as if something or someone was going to burst through the door in the other room.

He seemed to take it in stride. However, Ole and I jumped, and goosebumps ran along his arms as the hair on my hunches stood straight up. I let out a snarl to let Ole know that danger seemed to be lurking nearby, and we best consider a hasty retreat.

Ole took my hint as he said. "I think it might be best that your boiler should be looked at by a professional. It looks beyond my capability to fix it. Also, I remember you said you had an important appointment to attend to."

Carl: "You're right. I do believe the boiler needs an expert. We are taking up a collection to raise funds to fix it. As for my appointment, you are correct. I suggest we leave this dingy old place post haste."

Carl glanced at the door with the strange symbol with a worried look as he hurried us along. As soon as we had reached the top of the stairs and entered the sacristy, Carl quickly closed the door and locked it.

We were quickly ushered out of the church as Carl excused himself. As we stood outside the church, Ole looked over at me and said. "You know, Tesse, I have a feeling that there is something in the bowels of St. Catherine's that Carl doesn't want anyone to know about."

I gave Ole my raised eyebrow look and said. "Ya think? I'm pretty sure that there is more than meets the eye down there. After all, this is England. Ghosts and goblins. Longhall County, where the past lives and the present dies."

Ole: "You are one crazy dog. You want to walk through the graveyard and check out the old headstones. I bet some are really ancient and might just be your culprits down in the crypt."

"No. So what do you think made those strange noises down there? We were next to the boiler, and that wasn't it."

Ole: "For now, I don't care and don't want to know."

CHAPTER 14

After our visit to St. Catherine's, we figured that most of our exploring days in Longhall County and the Hedgehog Village had pretty well come to an end.

Fall was quickly approaching. The weather was cooling down, and Halloween decorations were popping up faster than mushrooms.

On what had become a regular habit, we were making our customary visit to Chaps Pub. Sitting at the bar listening to the local gossip, which we had begun to understand better as some of the local dialects and sayings were pretty foreign to our American ears. Today's discussion revolved around the removal of the old cork dart board from the wall and the rumor that Casey was now banning the traditional steel tip darts as they posed a danger of injury, and his insurance company had strongly suggested he switch over to the soft tip darts that were becoming so prevalent in the 'colonies.' Of course, the suggestion from his insurance company was made a bit more 'mandatory' for him, as if he did not get rid of the steel tip darts, his insurance rates would be going up.

Of course, this change was not something the old-timers were in favor of. Steel tip darts in pubs was an English tradition and not to be taken lightly. With this in mind, the change to soft-tip darts with electronic scoreboards was akin to 'sissy darts.'

Ole opted out of joining in on the darts discussion. He remembered steel tip darts when he was a kid, but in his later years, he actually sold and operated soft tip dart machines and had even played on 'heaven forbid' a soft tip dart league back in the 'colonies.'

To keep away from the 'steel versus soft tip' dart debate, Ole started pointing out some of the Halloween decorations that were on display in the pub. Old movie posters of the horror icons of the past were prevalent along the walls. He was soon explaining in very hushed tones the reasons he felt the Universal monsters from the 1930s and 1940s were better than the Hammer Studio versions that came later. Being in an English pub meant that if anyone overheard him, you can bet the arguments would have come in hot and heavy in favor of the local Hammer Studio monsters.

The last thing one would want to argue about was if Boris Karloff, Bela Lugosi, or Lon Chaney Junior were better horror icons than Christopher Lee or Peter Cushing. Casey happened to overhear Ole's comments to me, and he took it in stride as, being a dog owner, he knew that people often talked to their animals. As he refreshed our drinks, he commented to Ole that American horror movies were really great, but the English horror movies had much better and sexier-looking women in them. Ole had to agree to that.

The door of the pub opened, and the wind from outside caused the fake bats hanging from the ceiling of the pub to flutter their wings in the breeze. Kelley entered the pub pushing a two-wheeled cart that held a brand spanking new soft-tip Arachnid Fire dart board. The regular patrons of the pub grumbled and made snide comments about the 'sissy' darts as Kelley removed the old wall-hanging cork dart board, and then he gathered up the steel tip darts and put them in his toolbox so no one would use them on the new dart board. It seems steel tip darts thrown into a plastic electronic dart board would quickly be its death kneel. Kelley plugged the new machine's electric cord into an outlet on the wall, and it came to life with its opaque case lighting up in vibrant colors. That actually got a few ohh's and ah's from the pubs customers.

Archie: "You couldn't pay me to play darts using them, sissy plastic tip things you call darts. If they ain't got steel tips and wood barrels, they ain't real darts."

Kelley: "Archie, did you know this board will keep score for you ? No more writing your scores on the chalkboard."

Doug: "Archie won't like that; now he won't be able to cheat on his score."

Archie: "Listen here, you ol' body snatcher. I don't cheat. You just ain't good enough to beat me."

Kelley: "Now, now, gentlemen. No use to argue. I'll tell you what I'll do. I'm going to set this dartboard up for a dozen free games. You, gents, can try it out and see what you think. Just to sweeten the pot a bit, if you keep an open mind about the soft tip darts, I'll buy you all a round of beer."

Winton: "Free beer, I'm in."

Ray: "Me too. Noting tastes as good as a free beer. Winton and I will take on Archie and Doug. Losing team buys the next round of beers."

While the regulars were busy drinking beer and playing darts, Casey pushed the old piano from its prime spot on the wall to a back corner. Unfortunately, Archie noticed it.

Archie: "What you doing with the piano?"

Casey: "No one ever plays it anymore. It just sits here gathering dust. I've got something more modern coming in to take its place."

Archie: "What do you mean nobody plays it? That young'un of Henry and Nikki comes in here sometimes and plays it. You know, what's his name? Oh, yeah, Oscar, that's his name. He comes in every Christmas and plays it, and we all stand around and sing Christmas songs."

Casey: "That's the only time it gets played, a few days in December. That's it."

Before the discussion got any farther, the door opened, and in came Kelley pushing a jukebox which he rolled into the spot where the piano had been. The dart game temporarily stopped as the men stood staring at the round-topped Wurlitzer One more Time jukebox. Kelley plugged it in, and the revolving colored lights came on, and within a minute or so, the plastic pilasters began to bubble.

Kelley: "Behold your new source of music, gentlemen. You have 100 CDs to choose from. Each CD has anywhere from 12 to 24 songs on it. If you can't find something you want to listen to, then you really don't want to listen to anything."

Archie: "Just one more way to get our money, is all. What's the name of that thing? Wurlitzer. German, huh. That figures, they lose the war, and now they want us to buy their products and take our money."

Casey: "Archie, didn't your family originally come from Germany?"

Archie: "That's not the point. I was born in England, and my father served in the English Navy fighting the Nazi's. Not all Germans were Nazi's; a lot of them were good people doing what they had to do under an evil dictator. One thing for sure, the Germans know how to build things, so maybe a German Jukebox is all right."

Winton: "Archie, you may have been born in England, but you're still sour as sauerkraut."

That, of course, got a laugh from everyone in the pub.

Kelley quickly put some free plays on the jukebox and punched in some numbers to get the music started. 'Der Fuehrer's Face' by Spike Jones. This put everyone in the pub in an uproar as they started to sing along. Most of the joviality was aimed in good fun at Archie. At first, he sat sullenly with grumpy written all over his face. Finally, he took a big swig of his beer and started to laugh as he sang along.

The last big surprise Kelley wheeled in on his two-wheeled dolly was a Monopoly slot machine Kelley had added a light-up figure of Rich Uncle Pennybags to the top of the machine to add some class. He set the machine up alongside an old Allwin slot machine that depicted the Paul Boulton Defiant aircraft that was introduced in 1939 and had been used during World War Two at first as a daytime fighter and then more successfully as a night fighter. With the new Monopoly game set up and lighting up what at one time was a dark corner of the pub, it now added much-needed lighting to that area, and although it was much flashier than the old Allwin, it also cost a lot more than a penny to play. Of course, the rewards were also much better if you won.

The dart game temporarily came to a halt as the men came over to check out this modern-day era of gambling.

Archie: "Now that's more like it. You ain't taking away the old Allwin Defiant, are you?"

Kelley: "Nope. Casey said the old Allwin has been here since the war, and here it will stay. A reminder for all to see that England was victorious. This new game just gives you a more modern way to lose your money."

Ray: "That it will do." He then deposited the first of many coins that would follow into the machine.

Kelley went to the bar and sat down as Casey brought him a beer on the house.

Casey: "Free darts and music plus a bit of gambling, and I think we got the boys won over to the current century of games and entertainment. Plus, it will bring in some extra cash for both of us."

Kelley: "Well, almost to the current century. CD jukeboxes are a dying breed, it's all satellite music now, but for customers of your pub and of Hedgehoghaven, those 100 CDs should be just fine. They can see the CD being picked up and played just like the old 78 and 45 rpm jukeboxes. At their age they're still easily amused."

Casey: "That they are."

Ole and I just sat off on our own and enjoyed the banter of the local pub regulars. It was a good way for us to learn more about the people we now lived amongst.

The door of the pub opened, and in came Erica and her cousin Victoria. Erica led them on a bee line straight to us. The two girls plopped onto the bar stools flanking us.

Erica: "Hey Dad, can Victoria and I have some grape Nehi soda?"

Casey: "Just one each, and don't tell your mom I gave them to you."

Victoria: "Mister Ole. We're coming to your house on Halloween. Erica says you're going to take us to the castle to see the monsters."

Ole: "Erica, did you tell her that?"

Erica: "Well, you said someday you'd take us to see the castle. Halloween night would be the perfect time."

Ole: "I thought it was going to be just you and your sisters."

Victoria: "We're cousins. That's almost like being sisters."

Ole: "Did either one of you mention this to your parents?"

Erica: "Sure, they said it would be fine, seeing we would be going with Lord Ole."

Ole: "Just lay off on calling me 'Lord.' How about if we ask your dad if it's ok with him?"

Erica: "Looks like he's really busy right now. There's a lot of customers here. You can ask him later when he's not so busy."

Victoria: "Yeah, ask him later; much later after we've been to the castle would be a good time."

Ole: "Believe it or not, I was a kid once. I'll continue to think about it.

Erica: "You promised. Grown-ups never keep their promises."

Ole: "I'm not so sure I actually said I promised. If I remember right, I might have said I'll think about it. For right now, I think Tesse and I best be going home."

Erica: "See you on Halloween night."

Once we were back at our cottage and settled in, I looked over at Ole. "You have a problem on your hands. Erica is not the kind to forget. She'll be here on Halloween with her sisters and Victoria; you can bet on that. Just what are you going to do then?"

Ole: "Probably take a trip to the castle. I was a kid once. If I was those kids, I sure would like to see if there really are any monsters, and what would be more fun than going to a derelict castle then on Halloween night ? As for monsters, you and I both know there are no such things."

"But you have to remember we live in a county where 'Legends live, and Reality dies. The villagers have already told us that there are rumors of monsters living in the castle."

Ole: "The villagers were also amazed at a soft-tip dart machine."

"You going to ask permission from their parents before you take them to the castle?"

Ole: "I'm sure they'll get their parents' permission before they would actually ask me to take them there."

"Sure, like I'd ask permission to take a bone from a butcher's trash can."

Ole: "I think we should drop the whole monster castle thing and watch some television. How about we watch some reruns of Ballykissangel?"

CHAPTER 15

Halloween day. We woke to grey skies and a light drizzle of rain. Being just Ole and me, we didn't bother putting up any decorations. We never figured out our first Halloween in Longhall County and the fact that we were well away from any neighbors that we would have any trick-or-treaters. To hedge our bets, we decided to stay home for the day so as not to run into Erica, her sisters, or her cousin in the hope that they would forget about any trip to the castle or seeing any monsters. Being well off the beaten path, we figured we had a good chance of being left alone.

We did have one tradition that we brought with us from Minnesota, and we planned on keeping it. Every Halloween, we would make some popcorn and watch Universal Studios original 1931 version of Frankenstein. Of course, Boris Karloff as the Monster was the most memorable of the characters, Colin Clove did a nice job as Victor Frankenstein, but our favorite was Dwight Frye as Fritz.

The day stayed the same as it was in the morning; the only noticeable difference was that the drizzle had morphed into an early evening fog. Clouds moved across the night sky, allowing an occasional glimpse of a full moon. It was nearing 8 o'clock in the evening, and Ole had popped us his mother's old family recipe of butter popcorn with a sugar glaze. If you are not familiar with what we called sugar popcorn, think of caramel popcorn without the caramel.

Ole slipped the DVD into the player, and he settled into his recliner and put the foot pad up. I jumped up on Ole's lap and settled in with my bowl of water on the arm of the chair as Ole positioned his bottle of Squirt soda in the drink holder. He put our large popcorn bowl on the television tray that was attached to one of the recliner's arms. Ole turned off the lights to give a spooky atmosphere for our Halloween tradition of watching Frankenstein.

The movie was just starting when my dog's hearing picked up a sound from outside. It wasn't an animal or the wind. It was, yes, it was children.

Not just one or two of the little beasties but a whole herd of them the way it sounded. They were noisy and, as far as I was concerned, totally unwelcome. This was Ole and me time. How dare those little ragamuffins come roaming into our private space? Ole had not yet heard them. I figured they were not going away. In fact, they seemed to be getting closer. With the sound of the television drowning out their noise from Ole's ears, I resigned myself that he would find out they were here sooner or later, so I gave a warning bark to get Ole's attention. "I hear children, and I think they are coming to our cottage," I told him.

Ole: "Damn. I bet it's Erica and her sisters. Might even have her cousin Victoria with them. I was really hoping they would have forgotten about the castle. I suppose if they knock on the door, I'll have to answer it."

We sat dead still as Ole quickly turned the television off. With all the lights in the cottage off and no outdoor lighting on, we hoped the kids would think we were not at home and they might possibly leave the premises.

Of course, we would not be so lucky. One of the kids had a good hold on the door knocker and used it with such force and conviction that the sound reverberated throughout the cottage. Then things went silent for a little while. My dog, hearing, could pick up the squeaking voices of the children. They had seen the light from the television, and they knew we were home. I informed Ole that there was no way that we could just ignore them. Children have an ingrained sense that allows them the patience of Job from the bible when they really want something. It was of no use to hide. Ole would have to answer the door.

Ole took his time with the forlorn hope that the kids might give up and go home. He put a rubber stopper on his soda and put it back in the refrigerator. He shuffled to the door and slowly opened it. He did his best not to smile at the sight before his eyes. Nine mini-sized monsters and witches stood grouped together, and all at once, they assailed Ole with a very loud "Trick or Treat" with out-stretched arms holding plastic pumpkins and monster heads waiting to be filled. Treats were something Ole was not prepared for as he was so positive we would not see any trick-or-treaters so far from the village.

Ole: "Just a minute kids, and I'll get some treats."

He opened the refrigerator and reluctantly picked up his prized box of Reese's Peanut Butter cups, and went back to the door to pass them out. What really hurt Ole was that these were not those little bite-size one's that people usually dole out at Halloween. These were the big full-size two-pack one's that adults tended to hoard for themselves.

Once all the kids got their candy, Ole stood back to take a good look at them. He and I both recognized Tessa, Erica, and Olivia, who were dressed as the Sanderson Sisters from the movie Hocus Pocus. The other six were their cousins. Nikki and Henry's kids, Oscar, dressed as the Frankenstein Monster, while Elanor and Rosemary were dressed as Minions from the movie of the same name. Val and Kelley's girls had Caraline dressed as the Bride of Frankenstein, Victoria as a zombie cheerleader, and Kaylynn as a punk rocker with ripped jeans, a leather jacket, assorted chains dangling about, and multi-colored hair.

Ole: "You all look really scary. Great costumes. Now you best be off to collect more candy. I bet all the folks in the village can't wait to see your costumes."

Oscar: "We've already been to the village. You're our last stop."

Erica: "We've saved you for last so you could take us to the castle to see the monsters. Remember, you said you would take us."

Ole: "I thought it was just supposed to be you and your two sisters and maybe your cousin Victoria. Now instead of four of yours there are nine. I must admit it is a bit overwhelming, and I wasn't prepared to keep track of nine Halloween goblins at one time. I think maybe we should wait until we can get to just four at a time. Maybe next Halloween would be better; then I can be better prepared. "

Oscar: "We promise to be good. Tessa, Kaylynn and I will make sure the younger ones behave. Please, Lord Ole, please take us to the castle so we can see for ourselves if there really are monsters living there.

Then came a group plea from all the kids. "Pleeasse!"

Ole: "How many of you told your parents about this?"

Ok, it's Halloween. What a silly question, and it was met by a 'deathly' silence.

Ole: "None of you. Just like I figured , I was a kid once, a long, long time ago. If it was me and I was your age, I would have been up that mountain a long time ago, and I sure would not have told my parents because they would have stopped me. If they had found out later, I wouldn't have been able to sit down for a week, and I would have been grounded to my house for a month. However, all of you are here, and I hate to disappoint, so I guess I could pretend to be the responsible adult. I'll take you if you all promise to follow my rules and you don't breathe a word of this to anyone. Especially your parents. Understood?"

That 'deathly' silence once again hung in the air.

Ole: "I don't hear anyone promising to behave and not to tell."

Then as a group, we heard some loud and some barely audible 'I promise' coming from the group of assorted little monsters in front of us.

Ole excused himself to go and get his coat. He came back and proceeded to set down the rules for our adventure. "First off, there is a ladder and stairway that we will have to climb. If any of you are afraid of heights, you best go back home. I expect everyone to be very quiet and respectful of anything we might see. If there really are monsters there, we best stay out of their sight, and the last thing we want to do is to make any noise that they might hear and give away our presence. It might seem like we are peeping Toms, but better that than having some monster chasing us or eating any of you youngsters for their supper. If you have cell phones, turn them off now. No calls and defiantly no flash pictures or videos. Everyone is to stay together, no wandering off by yourselves. Last and most important, if I tell you to do something, you do it. No questions asked. Have I made myself clear?"

This time we got a resounding 'YES' from the group. The kids set their goody containers inside the cottage. Ole took the lead as we all trudged along the railway tracks to the ladder leading up to the Eastman mine. I took up the rear to keep any stragglers in line.

Once we reached the ladder, Ole sent Oscar up first and told him he should help the girls onto the rock ledge at the top. His job was to also make sure everyone stayed there until the rest of us had assembled. With no choice as to what to do with me, Ole went up last with me tucked into his jacket. Once at the top, Ole pointed out the castle keep off to the east. He then pointed the way to our destination. The castle looked scary and forbidding in the moonlight that was now shining as the clouds in the sky seemed to have disappeared as if to help us along on our quest.

Ole: "Ok, everyone is still here; that's a good sign. The castle keep is off to our right. The mine is to our left. If anyone should get separated from the group, remember these landmarks and get back here and wait by the ladder for the rest of us."

Oscar: "Unless you get captured by the monsters. Then you're on your own."

Ole: "Oscar, that's enough commentary from you. We are like the United States Marines. Their motto is 'no one gets left behind' unless, of course, it is Oscar."

Kaylynn: "That sounds good to me."

Everyone quietly laughed at that one.

Ole led us over to the steps that had been carved into the mountain many years ago leading up to the castle. He told me to take the lead. "Why me?" I asked

Ole: "You're small and won't be noticed so easily in case there really are any monsters roaming around. When you get to the top, take a good look around and find a place we can all go to that will hide us until we can get our bearings."

Caraline: "Do you always talk to your dog like he's a human?"

Ole: "Yes. He's defiantly smarter than a lot of the people I know."

Victoria: "Mom and dad talk to our dogs."

Rosemary: "So do my mom and dad."

Elanor: "Sometimes I think mom and dad like the dog more than they like us."

Oscar: "For sure, they like the dog better than they like you two. I'm their favorite because I was the firstborn."

Ole: "Everyone be quiet. Tesse is at the top of the stairs. Kaylynn, your next to go. There is no railing on the steps, so keep close to the side of the mountain and watch out for any uneven steps. The steps are old and worn, so be cautious."

Our caravan of children slowly made their way up the steps to the top. Once we had all reached the summit of our journey, I, as lead 'dog,' led everyone to an outcropping of rock that was big enough to hide all of us but still had a good view of the castle. I noticed some shadowy figures lurking about as I had been waiting for everyone. I quietly mentioned it to Ole that 'monsters' or at least something was definitely in the area.

As everyone's eyes adjusted to the dark, the shadowy figures began to take shape and could be recognized. Whispers among our charges filled our ears. "Look, it's Frankenstein's Monster and his Bride. I see the Creature from the Black Lagoon. There's a ghost in one of the castle's windows. I think that's Dracula on one of the parapets; wait, he's gone. There goes a bat. Up near the castles walls, there's a figure that looks like Bigfoot; look at him; I think he's peeing on a bush. I see the Mummy over there. He looks to be rewrapping some loose bandages on his hand.'

Tessa: "Lord Ole, can't we please take some pictures ? Our friends will never believe us if we don't have proof."

Ole: "No pictures. Remember the rules. You cannot tell anyone what you have seen here. It's our secret. If your parents ever find out, you will be grounded for life with no cell phones or computers. If the world ever finds out, our little village will never be the same. Reporters, scientists, and tourists would flock here like migrating birds and ruin our lives and our village forever.

Olivia: "That would be bad. I like our village just the way it is."

Olivia: "Look up. There's a bat!"

Then we heard the sound of a growl from behind us , the kids quickly gathered around Ole for protection as I stood in front of all of them, ready to defend my humans with my life. Right in front of us stood none other than the Wolfman, and he did not look to be in a friendly mood.

The bat that had been flying around was quickly forgotten as Ole bunched the kids behind him for their protection. He now stood face to face with the Wolfman.

The Wolfman stood his ground as he bared his teeth and growled. I told Ole I was with him; if it came to protecting the children, it would be Ole and me in a knock down drag-out fight, human and canine, against the wolf.

Before a confrontation could take place between us and the Wolfman, we heard a voice coming from behind us.

"Good Evening…my name is Dracula, Count Dracula from Transylvania. You may relax. Wolfman will stay at bay unless I tell him otherwise. May I inquire as to why you are in our domain?"

Ole had turned around to talk to our visitor as the kids now in front of him made their way behind him, not sure which place, front or back, was safer.

Ole: "The children were curious, is all. We mean no harm to anyone.

Dracula: "The children, they were curious. How about you and your dog? Were you two also not curious?"

Ole: "We were; I mean, we are."

Dracula: "Lord Long made a promise that we were free to live in the castle and roam its grounds as long as we did no harm to any of the residents of Longhall County. He also said that to the best of his ability that, no one would bother us. I know that Lord Long has passed from this earthly realm, and we of the castle have seen that you have moved into the Poacher's Rest. Is it safe for us to assume that you are now Lord of the County?"

Ole: "That is a safe assumption. I inherited the title from my great-grandfather. I'll do my best to honor his promise to you and those who live in the castle."

Dracula: "Why are these children dressed as witches and 'monsters' as people call us?"

Olivia boldly stepped forward and stood right in front of Dracula, hands on her hips and ready to speak her peace. "Well, you're dressed up too."

Dracula: "I am dressed properly as a 'Count' should be from my homeland in Transylvania."

Olivia: "Well, I'm dressed as Winifred Sanderson along with my sister witches Sarah and Mary from our homeland of Hocus Pocus."

Dracula: "Are you really witches? You seem very young to know very much about the dark arts."

Olivia: "Of course, we are not real witches. This is Halloween; we are dressed up for fun. I bet you're not a real vampire."

This was getting interesting, so Ole and I, along with the kids, stayed back to see where it would go.

Dracula smiled. "Look at my fangs. Don't they look real to you?"

Olivia: "No. You can buy fangs like that at any store around Halloween. I think I have a set just like them in my room at home with the rest of my toys."

Dracula knelt down on one knee in front of Olivia. "Toys, Nonsense. Here, try to pull my fangs off, but be careful not to prick your finger. The sight or smell of blood can make me lose control of myself."

Olivia: "You're funny, Mister Dracula."

Olivia took her fingers and pulled as hard as she could on one of his fangs. Then she tried again on his other fang. "They are real. Are you really the real live Dracula?"

Dracula: "I am."

By this time, most of Dracula's friends from the castle had gathered around to see what was going on. Many of them chuckle at Olivia's and Dracula's banter. Dracula introduced us to Frankenstein's Monster and his Bride, The Wolfman, who by this time had relaxed and was much less snarly, the Creature from the Black Lagoon, Bigfoot, the Werewolf, and a Ghost named Reginald who was at one time the Lord of some long forgotten castle, and the Mummy. There was also a white ghost who was fluttering around and seemed to be chasing his disconnected bottom half.

Rosemary: "Why is that ghost cut in two, and how come he is chasing his butt?"

Dracula: "Oh, him. He just came here late this afternoon. We don't usually accept many newcomers, but he was an inhabitant of Longhall County, so we made an exception. He owned the mine down below the castle. Seems he was ready to go home as the mine was shutting down for the day. He was going to board the train back to the village when he slipped and fell. The train started moving as he fell onto the tracks, and the wheels of one of the ore cars cut him in half. Right down the middle."

Caraline: "You mean everyone who dies in Longhall County is going to become a ghost and have to live in the castle?"

Frankenstein's Bride: "No, dear, not everyone. Only those who have done terrible things. Mister Eastman has overworked and underpaid his employees for years. He was about to sell the mine to an outside interest. The spirit of Lord Hall came back to make sure that didn't happen. Thus it will be that Mister Eastman may well have to chase his arse for eternity. Even here amongst us, he will always be an outcast to live in eternal damnation."

Frankenstein Monster. "It will be a lonely life for him, as it was for me before Doctor Frankenstein made me my lovely bride."

She kissed him and said. "It took me a while to see the inner beauty of my beloved husband."

Dracula: "It is time for all of you to go. You must promise us that you will never mention you were here or that you saw or spoke to any of us."

Creature in a gargling voice. "If you tell anyone, we will find you and bring you back to live with us. Forever."

Wolfman: "Or we could just eat you."

Just before the 'monsters' dispersed, I saw one of Dracula's concubines in the shadows. She suddenly turned into a bat and flew towards Ole, gently brushing his hand before she flew away. Ole and I then hurried the kids back to the stairway and then down the ladder for our trip back to our cottage.

Ole: "Well, you got to see what you wanted. Now remember to forget all about it and tell no one. Not your friends, not even your parents. Remember, the 'monsters' know who all of you are, and I would doubt that it would be pleasant if they came and took you away."

Olivia: "Lord Ole, they aren't really 'monsters,' are they?"

Ole: "Only to those who don't know or understand them. They're just different from what most people consider normal. So to those who are ignorant or selfish, they may seem like 'monsters.'"

Eleanor: "I think they were nice."

We arrived back at the Poacher's Rest, and Ole handed the kids their goody buckets. "All of you finally got to see what you wanted. Now remember to forget it and tell no one. Especially not your parents or I would probably be banished to the castle to live with our new friends up there."

After the kids were gone, Ole and I went back into our cozy, snug, and safe cottage. The Poacher's Rest never felt as homey as it does right now. Much safer than the castle on the mountain.

Ole retrieved his soda from the refrigerator and brought me a nice cold bowl of fresh water. We sat back down, turned our Frankenstein movie back on, and started munching on our popcorn. The movie took on a whole new meaning after our recent experience at the castle especially since we had now met the star of the movie in person.

About halfway through the movie, something dawned on me. "Ole, I saw a bat fly near your hand just as we were leaving the castle. What was that all about?"

"I believe it was one of Dracula's concubines. She slipped a note into my hand and then flew off."

I could see he was baiting me, but I figured what the heck, so I took the bait. "And what did the note say?"

Ole: "It said if I ever wanted a personal tour of the inside of the castle, she would be very happy to be my guide."

My turn to bait him. "Great, when do we go?"

Ole: "Are you crazy? First of all, she's a blood-sucking vampire. Second, she's one of Dracula's concubines. I don't think you would be too pleased to find me 'hanging' out with her. I sort of prefer to keep my blood in my body where it belongs."

"Well, you don't have a girlfriend. It never hurts to keep your options open."

CHAPTER 16

It was now the day after Halloween. To say we were glad Halloween was over would be a gross understatement. At least things had gone much better than expected with our meeting between the 'monsters' and the children. No one had been eaten or mauled. It would have been hard to explain to the kid's parents if we had lost any of their kids, especially if we had lost them to a bunch of 'monsters.' Now that I think about it, they weren't really 'monsters'; they were a lot like us. The movies had given the impression that they were dangerous or evil, and that's what stuck in the minds of most people. The real truth is that they just looked different then what most people would consider normal. They were outcasts from society who didn't fit the mold that society considered to be normal. They just wanted to be left alone in their own world with their own kind.

Of course, our biggest worry right now was about last night. There were nine children with us, and keeping nine mouths shut about last night's events might be a problem. One thing in our favor was that they were all related. So they would surely talk about what happened to each other, and hopefully that would satisfy their urge to share their adventures with each other and no one else.

It was getting late in the day when I suggested to Ole that we go to the village for supper.

Ole: "I don't think that's a very good idea."

"Why not?"

What if one or more of those kids from last night talked? If they told their parents or anyone else and word got around, we would have a lot of explaining to do. Constable Pete might just arrest us and toss us in jail for putting a minor in danger."

"Or, better yet, the villagers would grab their torches, hunt you down and burn you at the stake. I'm just an innocent little dog, so they wouldn't pay any attention to me. But I would miss you."

Ole: "Very funny. I think we should wait a few days just to be safe."

"What about Eastman? Don't you want to find out what happened to him? From what we were told at the castle, he's dead."

Ole: "He seemed like a nice guy. You're right. I am curious about how he died. Or did he die? Maybe telling us that story was just a way of scaring us off from any future visits to the castle."

"Even if they were, a ghost chasing his arse is a story worth investigating. Come on; we don't have to go to Chaps Pub if that's what has you all worried. We can grab some supper at Olive's Diner. After that, we can go next door to Rocky's Tavern for a drink."

Ole: "I suppose those two places would be safe enough. If there are any rumors about last night, we might be able to pick them up. Chaps has too many of the kids' parents hanging around, and I'd feel really uncomfortable there just in case any of those kids blabbed."

We hopped into our Norwegian Taxi and drove over to Olive's Diner. There were a few customers at the tables, but the counter stools were empty, so we opted for them. Figuring if we ate at the counter, we would be able to chit-chat with Olive and pick up any recent village gossip. With Olive being older, we were assured she had none of the kids from last night that would cause any problems.

Olive: "Ole and Tesse, nice to see you. I have bangers and mash with onion gravy on special today."

Ole and I looked at each other and figured what the heck, being from America but having been in England for a while, we had figured out that was just the English equivalent to American sausage on mash potatoes and, of course, onion gravy. We agreed it sounded like a good hearty meal. Seeing it was the day's special it took only a few minutes before our meal was in front of us, steaming hot and ready to eat. I got a bowl of water with mine, and Ole opted for a 7-up soda which was served in a bottle.

Things were slow in the restaurant, so Olive hung around by us and started in with some small talk.

Olive: "Did you hear the news about what happened to Eastman over at the mine yesterday?"

Ole: "We heard a rumor, but that's about it."

Olive: "Seems he slipped going down to the ore cars just as the train was pulling away from the mine. He landed on the railroad tracks and was cut sheer in half. Pretty bloody mess, so they say. Funny, he must have boarded those mine cars a thousand times. Must have been a freak accident is all. Oops. Not really something I should have said while you were eating. I'm sorry. Just for that, both your meals are on the house."

Ole: "That's not necessary. We'll pay. Got to help keep the local businesses going."

Olive: "Just between you and me, the rumor is that some of the villagers figured his death was a punishment from God. Everyone in the County knew how stingy he was paying his employees. He was a nice guy, so those that worked for him were very loyal, and they worked hard to make him money. However, the word is that he was in the process of selling the mine to an outsider. Employee loyalty, be damned, is the way it looked. He was going to make a boatload of money and leave all of those people who worked for him high and dry. That included some of the workers who had been with him for over 20 years. Plus, he even screwed over his very own nephew and grandson. I knew him, and he wasn't what you would call a God-fearing man. I, for one, and a lot of folks around here all agree with me and figure God got him for his evil ways. He put on a good front but his heart and soul were narcissistic."

Ole: "What do you suppose will happen to the mine now? You think the outsiders will still buy it?"

Olive: "Not much chance of that. His wife owns it now. She doesn't live around here. The two of them went their separate ways about a year ago. She's got herself a string of race horses and her own stables in another part of England. My guess is she will let her nephew Bubba and grandson Austin run it. The nephew has been working there for over 20 years, and he knows the operation inside and out. The grandson is more business oriented, so he'll most likely handle the finances.

Ole: "So what is the wife going to do?"

Olive: "Most likely stay with her stables. She loves those horses, probably a lot more then she loved him. She'll control the purse strings of the mine, and as long as money from the mine keeps coming in to support her and those horses, she'll be fine."

Ole: "I suppose a funeral will be taking place soon. Do you suppose he'll be buried at St. Catherine's?"

Olive: "That's a good question. You would have to ask Deacon Carl about that. Eastman wasn't what you would call a church goer. I think his wife will have him cremated and toss his ashes down a deep hole in the mine. She sure won't waste any of her money on a casket or a grave digger, and certainly not on a tombstone. Maybe she'll have a service for him just to appease their kids and the village. Although I doubt anyone cares anymore. After what he was about to do by selling out and screwing over his employees and relatives, I doubt anyone will even show up if they do have a funeral. Sad way to end your life by alienating everyone who once liked and cared about you."

Ole: "That it is."

Olive went over to check on her other customers while we kept eating. When she came back, she changed the subject to something less morbid, which was probably for the best.

Olive: "You didn't happen to be in the village last night, did you?"

Ole: "No. why?"

Olive: "Being Halloween night and with children running all over the place, it was thought best to keep the news of Eastman's death a secret so the kids would not be spooked and could enjoy themselves.

The only thing is that nine of the children, which just happened to be my grandchildren, disappeared for a few hours. Their parents had not seen them for quite a while, and they were getting worried. They called Constable Pete and Constable Queen Bee to keep an eye out for them. Luckily they finally turned up, but not before half the village was searching for them. They were questioned by their parents and even by Constable Pete, but all the kids would say was that they were playing in the woods and had lost track of time. Our village is pretty safe, and everyone looks after each other and the children, but you never know if a stranger might come here and cause a problem."

Ole gave me a smile to acknowledge that he felt much better that the kids had kept their mouths shut, and of course, it was good to know they all got home safe and sound. A tinge of guilt was felt by both of us for having caused worry for their parents and the village. It was also news to us that Olive was related to them.

Ole: "Well, I sure am glad to hear everything turned out all right with the children."

We finished our meal and went next door to Rocky's Tavern. It felt like a better place to relax as it was usually less busy then Chaps Pub, and we were pretty sure no one at Rocky's would be related to the kids and their families.

The only familiar face other than Rocky's that we recognized was Tony, who we had purchased our Norwegian Taxi from. He was sitting in a dark corner by himself, nursing what looked to be an assortment of shot glasses in front of him. He looked up and saw us, motioning for us to join him.

We sat down, and Rocky came over to take our order.

Rocky: "What's your pleasure, mates?"

Ole: "I'll have a pint of Two Women beer with a couple of green olives in it, and Tesse will have a bowl of Two Women straight up."

Rocky: "Maybe a dog treat on the side for the young lady?"

Ole: "That would be nice."

Tony: "Bring me another assortment of rum shots. Please."

Ole: "Tony, you already have 6 shot glasses in front of you, and some are still half full. What's the deal?"

Tony: "I just like trying different types of liquor. It's sort of a hobby for me. This week it's rum. I used to buy a few bottles of different flavors and types, but that was getting expensive, and if I didn't like one, it was a waste to throw or give it away. Rocky always seems to have a good assortment of almost everything, so I figured it was a lot cheaper to just buy a shot glass full of each brand and flavor and try them that way. I don't have to worry about getting liquored up and driving back to my shop as its close enough that I can walk there and sleep it off in my own comfy bed in my living space attached to the shop."

Ole: "I suppose you heard about Eastman?"

Tony: "I did. I'd feel worse about it if he hadn't been such a cheapskate. I had enough dealing with him over the years to know that getting money or even a thank you for a job well done was like trying to squeeze lemonade from a turnip."

Ole decided to change the subject. He and I both liked Eastman when we met him, but it seems he had one personality for those he wanted to impress and quite another personality for those who really knew him.

Ole: "Did you get many kids trick or treating at your place last night?"

Tony: "I did, and so did the fire station, but they came and went pretty quickly. I'll tell you that."

Ole: "Why were they in such a hurry? Trying to get as much candy as they could, I suppose?"

Or, my thought was that nine of them wanted get to our place and go monster hunting.

Tony: "St. Catherine's church is why. It's only two doors down from my place and right next door to the fire station."

Ole: "What was going on at St. Catherine's that would make any difference?"

I could see Tony had had a few too many rums as his eyes were glossed over, and he slurred his words a bit, but he did seem to be coherent and capable of reasonable thought and speech.

Tony: "Well, Deacon Carl doesn't decorate the church for Halloween. I bet there is some rule against it by the church. But, no matter. Last night there were screams and groans coming from either the church itself or maybe it was the graveyard. It was eerie as if they were coming from below the ground. Hard to say for sure. Whatever it was, it sent shivers up and down my spine, I can tell you that. Dale from the fire station came over to me, and we could both hear those sounds clear as day. They weren't coming from a loudspeaker, in case that's what you're thinking. We weren't even sure if they were human. Whatever it was, it sounded like it was chained up and trying to escape, or maybe it was just in extreme pain. I know there are ghosts in the village, but this was more like the cries of a banshee or something sinister and evil. Dale and I had heard the noises before, but never like they were last night. Maybe they were intensified as it was 'all hollow's eve' when the spirits came to call. It finally got so bad that we decided to call Constable Pete over to investigate."

Ole: "What did Pete have to say about that?"

Tony: "He said he stopped at St. Catherine's and talked to Deacon Carl about the strange noises. Carl told him it was just the old church furnace acting up due to the cool, damp weather."

Ole: "Did Pete believe him?"

Tony: "That's just what Pete asked him. Pete said he didn't want to doubt the word of a man of the cloth. However, he did say he would like to take a look at that boiler under the church. Seems he is not sure just how far his authority goes in such a matter. Longhall County, as you know, is sort of an anomaly in England, and we pretty much govern ourselves. In most cases, it would be all he needs to investigate, being the law and all. But the Church, now that might just be a whole other matter. It is still a hold out from the old days and sort of a law unto itself. My bet is that you, as Lord of the County, might just have to make a decision as to how much authority the law in Longhall County has to investigate something happening on church property."

Ole: "Lord of the county, you say? I assume you figure it's up to me to decide what can be done?"

Tony: "Your bloody right on that account, mate."

I could see Ole wanted to turn tail and run. However, he really is Lord of Longhall County, whether he likes it or not. Just how much authority that entailed, he really didn't know. Ole probably had the authority to order an investigation into almost anything that might jeopardize the wellbeing of the county or its inhabitants. Yet, to have enough authority to override the sanctity of the Church was a whole other matter.

The door of the tavern opened, letting in a bright light to our dimly lit corner. A large, almost giant-like figure stood in the doorway with his back blocking much of the brightness of the world outside the dark insides of Rocky's little tavern. His features were shadowed in the darkness that surrounded the front of his body. His size and the shape of his cap made him quickly recognizable as none other than Constable Pete.

Once he closed the door, he became more human as his features were now visible. He looked around the room until his eyes finally settled on Ole and me.

Pete said, "I'll have my regular" to Rocky as he headed towards our table. He took a seat and looked at Tony as he said. "Tony, I bet you have someplace to be other than here. Don't you?"

Tony: "Now that you mention it I probably do. We'll be seeing you three later."

Rocky soon appeared with two pints of beer which he set down in front of Pete, along with a bowl of chips. Pete popped a handful of chips into his mouth and washed them down with a large swig of beer.

Ole: "Pete, you're in uniform. Are you still on duty?"

Pete: "In this village, with me and Queen Bee being the only law, I'm always on duty. She's too darn flighty and mean to be in charge, so it's up to me to be on call 24 hours a day. You did catch my little pun there, didn't you? Queen 'Bee' a little flighty, get it?"

Ole: "Yeah, I got it. You know where I come from, an officer or, in your case, a Constable wasn't allowed to drink while on duty."

Pete: "Listen, mate, this isn't the colonies. It's England, the British Isles. In fact, it's not even so much England or the British Isles as it is Longhall County, and things, as you should know by now, are a bit different here than anywhere else in the world. As for drinking on duty, it's just beer; here in Longhall County and most of the British Isles, having a beer is no different than having a glass of lemonade back in the colonies."

Ole: "Besides beer-guzzling on duty, don't you think your treatment of Tony was a bit on the rude side?"

Pete: "I don't mince my words with criminals or friends. Anyways Tony's used to me. He knows I didn't mean any harm. Ol' dead Eastman treated Tony a lot worse than I ever have. Heck, Tony was always fixing stuff for him at darn near cost, and Eastman still complained about the cost and never once gave Tony so much as a thank you. I treat Tony like an angel compared to Eastman."

Ole: "Ok, let me get this straight. You are a beer-drinking angel of a constable. You come in here, toss out the fellow I'm drinking with, and bad mouth a dead man. Just what is the point of all of this?"

Pete: 'Oh yeah, the point. We were having so much fun bantering that I all most forgot why I was looking for you. Did you happen to hear what happened on Halloween night?"

This was not sounding good for Ole and me. I quickly told Ole to keep his mouth shut and just listen. Maybe Pete didn't mean what we had been up to with the kids. It might be something else, so no need to incriminate ourselves so early in the game.

Ole: "I heard a few things. You talking about Eastman dying?"

Pete: "No, why would I want to talk about that, mate? It was just a tragic accident, could have happened to anybody. I'm talking about the other thing that happened that night."

Ole: "You mean about a bunch of kids that had gone missing for a few hours?"

Pete: "No! Who told you that?"

Ole: "Olive over at the diner mentioned that her grandkids had disappeared for a few hours on Halloween night, and no one knew where they were."

Pete: "Sure, a bloody grandma getting all worked up over nothing. Kids are kids, they wander off for a little while, and everyone gets all worked up."

Ole: "So, what are you talking about?"

Pete: "The noises coming from St. Catherine's."

Ole: "Yeah, Tony said something about that. I also seem to remember Dale at the fire station mentioned it to me some time back about strange noises coming from either the graveyard or the church. Why the sudden interest now?"

Pete: "There's been rumors of the strange sounds coming from, as you said, either the graveyard or the church for some time. The locals like to claim it is ghosts or restless spirits. Not such an unusual thing to hear about in England. However, now I seem to have a problem. Before the sounds were mostly heard by the fireman on duty and an occasional passerby. But being Halloween night, there were a lot of kids alone and with their parents and, of course, an assortment of partygoers, especially those coming from Rocky's tavern as it's so close to St. Catherine's. Of course, there were also a lot of folks wandering around after drinking too much at Chaps Pub that were heading to Rocky's for just a bit more to drink.

The one that really piqued my interest was Doug from the clothing-funeral shop when he called to say he heard the same scary noises while he was upstairs in his bedroom over his shop. He told me they sent shivers down his spine. Just think about that. A mortician getting the shivers from ghosts at the church. Doug spends a lot of time with the dead, so if he gets spooked, it's time to investigate."

Ole: "I think it's great that you are taking this seriously, and I applaud your bravery in going over to St. Catherine's to check it out. Carl gave me a tour of St. Catherine's a while back, and I mentioned the rumors of strange sounds, but he did his best to brush them off. I wish you the best of luck when you try to talk Deacon Carl into letting you roam around his church."

Pete: "Did you hear anything unusual during your tour of the church?"

Ole: "Now that you mention it, we did. Tesse's ears perked up at the same time I heard it. Strange noises coming from below the church. Seems there is an old crypt beneath the church, and it is now used for the church's furnace. I mentioned the noises to Carl, but he said it was just the old boiler acting up. I did some work with a boiler at one of my old jobs back in the colonies, so I offered to take a look at the boiler, thinking I could help out with the problem. Carl was hesitant, and it took a bit of persuading, but he finally let Tesse and me go down to the crypt area to check it out."

Pete: "Was the boiler ok?"

Ole: "It needs a lot of work; it wasn't heating the church when we were there. If it had been working with a full head of steam, Tesse and I would have high-tailed it out of there. That boiler is anything but safe. I suppose Carl figures a few prayers, and God will keep him and his parishioners safe. Hopefully, for them, God sends the church a good boiler repair guy before winter sets in."

Pete: "Forgot about the boiler. Did you see or hear anything suspicious while you were there?"

Ole: "We did. There was a door off from the boiler made of heavy wood, and it had strange, almost satanic-looking symbols by it. I'm not positive, but I think both Tesse and I heard human-like sounds, something like whimpering or moans, and maybe even the faint rattling of chains coming from behind that door. Before I could ask about it, Carl rushed us back up the stairway and into the church. He was reluctant to talk about what we told him we heard, and he quickly sent us on our way."

Pete: "You heard suspicious noises that might have been human in a crypt beneath a church, and you didn't think that maybe you should have told me about it?"

Ole: "It may have crossed my mind. I don't really remember. I do remember that I thought something suspicious was going on down in the crypt. I even remember saying to Tesse that someday we should investigate things further."

Pete: "So you're telling me that you told your dog something seemed suspicious but not the police?"

Ole: "Yeah, that seems to sum it up."

Pete: "You trust telling your dog things more than you trust the police?"

Ole: "Of course, that only makes sense, doesn't it?"

Pete: "Let's move on a bit. From what you just told me and the disturbances that were heard at St. Catherine's on Halloween night, I'd say it is about time we have a good talking with Deacon Carl about that crypt beneath the church. Don't you?'

Ole: "Yes. However, I think I need to correct you about something."

Pete: "What?"

Ole: "You said 'we.' You must mean 'you' as you are the Chief Constable of Longhall County. Unless, of course, that 'we' meant you and Constable Queen Bee."

Pete: "Are you daft? Queen Bee is crazy nuts. She's fine when it comes to vehicle violations or chasing kids out of trash bins, but that's about it. I mean you, me, and of course, your dog Tesse are going to see Deacon Carl and get to the bottom of this." Pete let out a hardy laugh. "Get it? Crypt, underground. Get to the 'bottom' of this."

Ole smiled, and I gave a tail-wagging laugh. It was actually a pretty good pun.

Ole: "Me? Why me and Tesse? You're the law in Longhall County. It's your job. It's none of our concern."

Pete: "That's where you're wrong. This is England, and we have to follow most of their laws, but as you pointed out, this is Longhall County. From the very beginning, Longhall County has always sort of bent the laws of England to fit our needs. Your forefathers made sure that only 10 laws were to be strictly enforced in the County. These 10 laws are none other than God's Ten Commandments.

You shall have no other Gods before me.

Thou shall not make unto thee any graven images.

Thou shall not take the name of the Lord thy God in vain.

Remember the Sabbath day and keep it Holy.

Honor thy father and thy mother.

Thou shall not kill.

Thou shall not commit adultery.

Thou shall not steal.

Thou shall not bear false witness against thy neighbor.

Thou shall not covet.

The problem you and I have is that we are dealing with the church. Religion has long held sway in England and even here in Longhall County. The Church is still pretty powerful and not to be messed with any more than absolutely necessary.

You being Lord of Longhall County, have the authority to tell Deacon Carl that it is necessary from a legal standpoint that we search the crypt of the church as there may be something there that could disrupt or endanger the village of Hedgehoghaven or maybe even the whole County."

Ole: "What if I don't want the authority to do that?"

Pete: "I suppose you could refuse. Of course if there really is something in that crypt and it gets out and hurts someone you would have to carry the guilt of what happened for the rest of your life. Plus, it would probably turn everyone in Longhall County against you. As long as anyone can remember, Longhall county has been a peaceful quiet place to live and bring up a family. The Lord of Longhall County has always been respected as someone who is fair and will make every effort to do what is right for the majority of the people who live here. What do you say, let's search the crypt and lay to rest any rumors that surround the noises coming from St. Catherine's."

I looked at Ole, who I knew was in a quandary over this situation. I told him that, like it or not, he had accepted his inheritance, and that meant he had also agreed to all the responsibilities that came with it. If Pete said he needed Ole's backing to handle the situation, then the only option available was to buck up and hit the problem head-on. At least having Pete at his side was an advantage. Pete is a big guy, and if there is anything that might cause us harm in the crypt, all Ole and I would have to do is hide behind Pete and let him take the brunt of the attack and then run for our lives.

Ole: "When are you planning on talking to Deacon Carl?"

Pete: "I already have. I set up a meeting with him at seven o'clock tonight."

Ole: "You mean you told him we wanted to see the crypt, and he agreed?"

Pete: "No, you think I'm an idiot. If I had told him that, he would never have agreed to meet us. I just told him I had something I wanted to talk to him about. I'm a good Christian, so my assumption is that he figured I wanted to make some kind of confession or something. I bet once we get there and he finds out what we want, it will darn near scare him right out of his ecclesiastical underwear."

Ole: "You do have a bit of a mean streak in you, don't you?"

Pete: "Not really; let's just say I have a mischievous side."

Ole and I left Rocky's and went back to our cottage to relax for a while before our meeting with Deacon Carl.

CHAPTER 17

It was time. Seven o'clock was fast approaching, and we needed to leave the cottage and head to St. Catherine's for our meeting with Pete and Deacon Carl. Ole and I were both moving in slow motion, trying our best to not really have to do this but it wasn't going to make any difference; we were just prolonging the agony. We knew what our duty was, and we were duty-bound to keep it come hell or high water. I figured we were more likely facing hell than high water before this was all over.

We pulled into the parking lot and saw Pete leaning against his white and blue police car, waiting for us. He was warily eyeing St. Catherine's. I could tell he was as reluctant as we were for the upcoming confrontation with Deacon Carl. Don't get me wrong. Carl is a super nice guy, but his job is to protect his church and guide his flock.

Pete: "Ole, Tesse, you two ready to meet your maker?"

Ole: "Well, I don't think Deacon Carl is our maker, and hopefully, things won't get that serious."

Pete laughed. "I hope they don't, but I've seen a lot of horror movies, and crypts give me the willies."

Ole: "Me too."

It didn't help that it was getting dark out, and fog blanketed the ground like a 1970s shag carpet from a bad movie. Glancing over at the graveyard with its tombstones poking up from the ground like Satan's fingers made things seem even more eerie than they already were.

Before we could get to the front door of the church, we stopped dead in our tracks as a mysterious figure came towards us from the graveyard. It was of average height, and a dark hood covered its head. With the hood up, all we could make out was a dark shadow where a face should be. In one hand, the figure was carrying a long-handled scythe. The three of us stopped as Ole muttered. "It's the Grim Reaper himself, and he's coming our way. Pete, I hope you have a gun."

Pete: "I don't carry a gun unless I know that I'm going up against someone else that has one."

Ole: "That's all right, I've got my Schofield revolver with me. Just so you know, we'd feel a lot safer with you in front of Tesse and me."

Pete: "You do know that it's illegal for you to have a handgun in England unless you are licensed to do so. Just for my own information, where did you get a revolver?"

Ole: "First of all, this is Longhall County. Remember the place that bends the rules. Secondly, if it really matters, I smuggled it over from the colonies. It belonged to one of my relatives that roamed the Wild West; they called him Buffole. Seems my solicitor got the luggage I had through customs with no questions asked. I guess it helps to be a Lord in England. Do you think a bullet will stop the Grim Reaper?"

Pete: "If that really is the Grim Reaper, I don't think shooting it will do much good. My guess would be it's already dead."

Multi-colored lights coming from inside the church filtering through the stained glass windows was all we had to see as the figure came ever closer. The hair on my haunches stood up, and I bared my teeth in readiness to protect my partner Ole.

The figure was almost upon us when it pulled down its hood to reveal none other than Deacon Carl.

Pete: "You gave us a bit of a fright there, Carl. There for a moment, we thought you might be 'Death' itself looking for a few new souls to take. By the way, what's with the hood and the scythe in your hand?"

Carl: "Oh, that. The hood is because it's so cool and damp. The scythe, I was using that to cut down some of the taller weeds in the grave yard. I like to do it after dark so that people will not think I am being un-respectful of their dearly departed doing it in the daylight hours. Sorry for the scare. I guess I forgot about our meeting until I saw the lights on your vehicles as you pulled into the parking lot."

Pete: "The reason I called this meeting is that there is a situation here at St. Catherine's that has been brewing for some time now. It seems to have come to a head on Halloween night."

Carl: "Really? A situation, you say. Something so important that it involves an investigation by not only the police but also by the Lord of Longhall County and his dog Tesse?"

Pete: "It does. Do you suppose we could go inside and talk things over? It's a bit chilly out here?"

Carl: "Of course. There are no parishioners here at this hour; as you just said, it is too cold and damp for most of them to leave their snug little cottages. By the way, I would like to say it is quite a blessing to see you here. I see so little of either of you at Sunday services, especially you, Ole. I do not believe I have ever seen you here for services since you moved here. If you feel you cannot leave Tesse home alone, she would be welcome to attend with you. As for Pete, he and his family show up occasionally. Of course, it's usually just for someone's wedding or a funeral."

Ole: "It's not that I don't believe in God. It's just that I'm not a big fan of organized religion. Any time you put humans in charge of something, they tend to slant things to their way of thinking, and that does not always coincide with what the bible teaches."

Carl: I do have to agree with what you just said, but what is important is the fellowship of others who do believe and trust God and follow his commandments."

Pete: "We could argue the pros and cons of this all night. That's not what we are here for."

Carl: "Exactly what are you here for?"

Pete: "The strange noises."

Carl: "Strange noises? What strange noises?" I have no idea what you are talking about."

Pete: "Come on, Carl, you must have heard them. I've had folks telling me they sound like everything from whimpers to screams, and even the rattling of chains. This has been going on for some time, but it seemed to be even more pronounced on Halloween night. Enough so that it scared the kids and even some of the adults. I know this is England, and hauntings and strange happenings can be fairly common, but when the villagers start to complain, I have to investigate."

Carl: "Ole, you being the Lord of Longhall County, do you condone Pete's behavior on this matter? After all, this is a house of God, and it is a sanctuary for any who need it."

Ole: "Does your sanctuary include the 'undead' or their spirits? I'm afraid I have to agree with Pete on this."

Carl: "Undead? Spirits? You two are talking nothing but nonsense. You can't actually believe what a bunch of kids or superstitious villagers say."

Pete: "As it may be. We would like to pay a visit to the church's crypt."

Carl: "First of all, it is not a crypt. It is the church's boiler room. Second, I think I would like to see a warrant that allows you to make any search of church property legal."

Pete: "Carl, I have the Lord of Longhall County with me. If I was to ask for a warrant, he is in the position to legally grant it to me. So all this legal nonsense aside, I suggest you just be polite and accommodate our request."

Carl knew that no matter how much he argued, he was not about to win. He finally shrugged his shoulders and said, 'so be it.' He then reluctantly led us to the stairway leading to the boiler room.

We carefully descended the stairway as we had done when Carl had given us a tour of the church. Once we reached the bottom, Carl ushered us away from the room with the locked door and its painted symbols into the boiler room.

Carl: "Well, this is your demon or ghost or whatever that makes all the strange noises and rattling of chains that you've heard about. It's old and cranky and needs to be replaced someday if the church finances permit it. Pete, maybe you would like to arrest this old boiler monster and haul it off to jail. You're a big guy, it might just be you can hoist it up and carry it on your back up the steps and strap it to the top of your police car."

Ole whispered to Pete: "We need to find out what's behind the door in the other room. I'm sure Tesse and I heard noises coming from there the last time we were here."

Pete: I may look big and gullible, and I am a big guy, but I'm not that gullible. You and I both know that old boiler doesn't scream and whimper like a human or an animal, for that matter. It may rattle a bit, but that's about all. We want to see what's behind the door in the other room."

Carl: "It's just an old Crypt. Legend has it that the foundation of the church was laid on top of the crypt. How many centuries before it was constructed, no one knows. Possibly the Druids built it and retreated underground as they were being hunted by the Christians. There is also a rumor that it may have been used to torture non-believers or traitors to the kings over the years. You know, it was not unusual for major structures like churches to be built on existing foundations to save money and time. If you want my opinion, I do not believe it would be wise for us to go in there."

Pete: "Why not? You don't have anything to hide, do you?"

Carl: "It's not necessarily that I have something to hide. That chamber is centuries old. It is not safe to venture in there. It could collapse at any moment."

Ole: "Carl. Pete brought me along because, as Lord of the County, I had to give him authorization to do what he feels is best. Basically, I represent his search warrant for the premises. Church property or not, this building is located in Longhall County, and if something strange is going on in the crypt, we mean to get to the bottom of it. Church property or not, we are going in. Now, you can find the key to the door and cooperate with Pete's investigation, or we can break it down. It's up to you."

Carl's face turned white which was in huge contrast to the black outfit he was wearing. He fidgeted around a bit, and then he finally stammered out the words. "All right. I'll take you into the crypt. I warn you; you are not going to like or even understand what you are about to see in there. Remember, you have been warned."

Ole was wearing his Sherpa-lined denim coat that covered the holster with his Schofield revolver under it. I saw him touch the revolver and flip off the leather hammer strap that held it in place. He was definitely preparing for the worse scenario.

Pete tapped the collapsible baton on his belt with his hand to make sure it was at the ready.

Carl opened a small wood cupboard near the door and reached up into the very back corner near the top of the cupboard, and retrieved an aging old skeleton key. He put it into the lock and juggled and fumbled with it until we heard the lock click open.

Inside the door was a ledge that held an old kerosene lamp. Carl took a match from the shelf and lit the lamp.

Carl: "Follow me and be very careful. The floor here is made of stone and slants downwards until we come to some stairs. The dampness down here can make walking quite treacherous

We followed Carl until we came to another heavy steel door with a small square barred window so you could peek inside, which we did, but it was to no avail as the room behind the door was pitch black. Carl once again fumbled with his key until he got the door open. Its rusty hinges groaned as he pushed the door open. There was another shelf and another kerosene lamp which Carl lit to give light to the room.

Even in the dim light, what we saw was a shocking sight. This was not so much a crypt as a torture chamber. Although there were most likely bodies behind the stone makers with dates embedded into some of the walls, there were other things that may have caused the demise of some of those individuals.

There were manacles attached to chains that were imbedded into the stone walls. Wooden racks and stocks to lock down a person's neck, arms, or legs were scattered about the room. An iron maiden, now rusted through in spots, revealed the spikes inside that were just long enough to pierce the skin and start the process of being bled to death. A wooden rack with manacles for a person's wrists and ankles was set up to stretch a body until the joints would be torn apart. A fire place long dormant had metal pokers and branding irons that would have been heated until red hot and used to extract confessions; whether truth or lies, was left to the judgement of those in control. A shelf was lined with metal boots used to crush a foot and a metal mask with spikes to poke out eyes. Finger crushers and tongue extractors were only a few of the horrible instruments of torture that were all about this evil domain.

Carl: "There you have it. The torture chamber. Now that you have seen it, we can be on our way."

Ole: "I thought you said it was a crypt?"

Carl: "It is. You can see there is a chamber for bodies along the walls with markers for those who are entombed here. As we leave, if you look along the walls going up the way we came, you will see iron and marble stone markers. These mark the bodies of some who have devoted their lives to the church or those who, for whatever reason, had no place in the common graveyards. The practice of entombing people in these crypts was abandoned centuries ago."

Pete: "What about the torture chamber? Who built and used it?"

Carl: "It is not known to me, and no information about it was passed onto myself or my predecessors as far as I know. Let's just say it is a mystery."

Ole: "Didn't the church sometimes use torture to get confessions from those they thought might be witches or heretics?"

Carl: "Those were different times during the Middle Ages. It was not common practice until the end of the 16th century and early 17th century, particularly with the succession of James VI to the throne. King James showed interest in the witch trials of 1589 to 1590 that took place in Scotland. When he succeeded to the English throne in 1603, he sharpened the English Witchcraft Act the following year.

Witch trials were most frequent in England in the first half of the 17th century. The 1640s to 1650s were the most intense when witch hunters such as Matthew Hopkins plied their trade. Contrary to popular belief, most who were charged with witchcraft were not burned at the stake unless the charge also contained other offenses that were against the law, such as treason or murder. In most cases, if one was found guilty of witchcraft, they were hung by the neck until dead. The witchcraft act of 1735 finally ended the prosecutions for alleged witchcraft."

Ole: "Great bit of history, Carl, but you seemed to have skirted my original question about the church's involvement in the prosecution and killing of alleged witches."

Carl: "Yes. Oftentimes, a senior member of the church would be involved in examining and questioning those accused of witchcraft."

Ole: "I think I would like to explore the torture room more thoroughly, if you don't mind?"

Pete: "I think that's a great idea."

Carl: "You have already seen all there is to see. It's not safe down here. The place is centuries old, and the walls and ceilings are crumbling. I think we should best be on our way."

We heard a noise from somewhere near the torture chamber. Pete, Ole, and I quickly left Carl standing by himself as we went to investigate. A scraping sound of chains and a slight whimpering was traced to a large tapestry of a bearded man that had on a large hat, and tall boots and was dressed in a clothing style from the 1600s. The name 'Matthew Hopkins' Witch Finder General 1620-1657, was embroidered along the top.

The three of us stood silently in front of the tapestry as we strained our ears to listen. Me being a canine, was the first to pick up the whimpers of what sounded human, and I quickly relayed the information to Ole.

Ole: "Pete, there's whimpering coming from behind that tapestry."

Carl overheard Ole and was quick to discount what he had said. "It's nothing, just rats. The old place is full of them."

Pete: "All the same, I think we should take a look behind the tapestry." He pulled the tapestry off to the side to reveal a heavy iron door with no window and a large sliding metal bolt that was pushed into the wall and padlocked so that nothing that was behind that door could possibly escape.

Ole: "Carl, what's behind this door?"

Carl: "I have no idea. I didn't even know it was there. I'm sure it is of no consequence. You should go back upstairs to the church and forget all this nonsense about spooks, ghosts, or witches. Or whatever you two think you are looking for."

Pete: "Really? You had no idea at all that this door was here? I suppose you are going to tell me that you don't have a key to open this lock? Think really hard, Carl. Maybe it just slipped you're mind. When we get this door open, and I don't mean if, I mean when it might just be best if you cooperate and tell us everything you know. If there is something sinister going on behind this door and you have any knowledge of it, I would strongly suggest you speak up right now. If not, I would hate to think what your parishioners would think or say about you if I have to arrest you and put you behind bars."

Ole: "Pete, would it be inappropriate of us to use some of this torture equipment to help Carl jog his memory?"

Pete: "That might be fun. I think we should stoke up a fire and hang him from the wall. A few hot pokers in strategic places on his body might make him very cooperative. It might even jog his memory as to where the key to this locked door is."

A blood-curdling scream suddenly pierced the air. All of us froze in place. There was no doubt it came from behind the locked door.

Pete went over to Carl and grabbed him by the scruff of the neck, and drug him over by the chain manacles hanging from the wall. He told Ole to light a fire and get the hot pokers ready. He pulled Carl's hands over his head and was about to clap the manacles onto Carl's wrists. "No more games, Carl. Time for us to get serious."

Carl: "Hold on, mates! My memory is coming back to me. Before I say any more, you have to give me your word that you will listen to what I have to tell you. You need to understand the circumstances and my position as a Christian and an esteemed member of the clergy as to how this situation needed to be handled."

Pete released his grip on Carl. Carl walked over to the door that was behind the tapestry. He ran his fingers along the top of the iron rail that held the tapestry in place until he felt the key that was hidden there. He unlocked the door and lit it swing open. A faint flicker from a candle's flame barley lit up the room.

We stepped into the room, which had a cold stone floor and stone walls. Carl mumbled. "I did what I could for her. I left her candles and matches and I bring her food twice a day. You have to realize she is more a demon animal than a human."

Chained to the wall and cowering like a wild, scared animal, we could make out the figure of a small in stature woman dressed in the tattered remnants of a nun's habit.

Ole: "Carl, what the hell is wrong with you?"

Pete: "You've got a lot of explaining to do. Holding someone against their will is one thing. Torturing them and chaining them up in a dungeon is something else altogether."

Ole: "I would have never imagined in my wildest nightmare that you were capable of doing something like this."

I started to walk towards her, thinking that maybe as a sweet-looking little dog she might feel a sense of safety with me. As I came within her reach she lashed out at me with jagged fingernails that would have slashed through my fur and drawn blood if I hadn't jumped out of her reach at the very last second.

Carl: "Please let me explain. It's not what you think."

Pete: "You have no idea what I'm thinking. I very much doubt that you can come up with any sort of rational explanation. However, I'll gave you sixty seconds to do so. If I don't like what I hear, what you've done to this poor woman will be nothing compared to what I am preparing to do to you."

Carl: "Remember the Longhall County moto. 'Where legends live, and reality dies.' Well, not all legends are good ones. This poor creature came to me disguised as a nun. She called herself Sister Theresa. She told me she had come from a convent far away from here and that she was confused and lost. She could not even remember the name of the convent or that of any of the sisters that she had been associated with. She was scared and felt she was losing her faith in God."

I, of course, took pity on her and allowed her sanctuary. I even let her move into the spare room in my cottage. For a few days she helped me around my cottage and in the graveyard where she seemed to be the most comfortable tending to the graves and placing fresh flowers on those that had been neglected for years. She even weeded along the stone walls of the graveyard and seemed be more comfortable tending to the dead than associating with the living.

When I asked her if she might not feel more at home helping to clean and arrange things inside the church, she shied away. I finally convinced her to enter the church with me so that she might say prayers. Once we entered the church she refused to pray. As we approached the cross with Jesus on it she shirked out that she was a child of Satan and she would destroy me and all that was holy. She lunged at me and her eyes and fingernails turned black as she tore at my face and clothes and caused gashes on my arms and hands that were now oozing blood.

I managed to throw her off me, and she slammed into the side of the pews. Then she crawled on her hands and knees to where some of my blood had dripped onto the floor and started to lap it up with her tongue like a crazed wild animal. I stood in horror watching her. Then she sat up and licked some of my blood from her finger tips as she glared at me and said. "I am Satan's offspring and I have come here to destroy you and your church and all who believe in your God."

I wasn't sure what to do, so I prayed to God to give me the strength to subdue this creature of darkness and save my church and its followers from this evil. She got on all fours and began to lap up more blood from the floor. Seeing my chance I jumped onto her back with her body pinned face down and flat to the floor I took off my leather belt and bound her hands behind her back. All the time while I was doing this she kept thrashing her head back towards me trying to bite me. I now noticed her teeth had turned into fangs red with my blood she had licked from the floor. I wasn't sure what to do with her. I knew if I called the law they would not believe me. Using my belt I drug her down here. All the while she screamed out cuss words and words totally foreign to any but the Devil spewed from her mouth. I had discovered this hidden room years ago but never imagined I would have any use for it. There you have it. If you wish to charge me with a crime so be it. Then I can wash my hands of this evil and she will be your problem."

Pete: "Just how long did you plan to keep her here?"

Carl: "I was waiting for an answer from God. Or at least a visit from my superiors to see how they wanted to handle this. If this was still in the days of the witch trails I have no doubt she would have been found guilty and hanged. However we are supposed to be more enlightened about things like this nowadays."

Ole: "Did it never cross your mind that she might just be mentally unstable."

Carl: "You did not witness what she turned in to. Mentally unstable people cannot change the color of their eyes, grow pointed finger nails or fangs for teeth. I tell you, she is a prodigy of Satan."

Pete: "Child of Satan or not we can't leave her here like this. We'll have to take her out of here and get her to a psychiatric hospital."

Theresa looked at us with pleading eyes. I had never seen a creature or a human being who looked so helpless and lost. "Please help me. Release me from these chains and set me free. Carl lies. He is evil just like all of his kind. They preach righteousness but look how he treats a poor nun. A child of his flock. He is the one who deserves to be chained up and punished in this dungeon. Not poor innocent me. Punish him!"

I looked at Ole, Ole looked at Pete, and Pete looked at Carl.

Pete: "I'm not sure how to handle this. Although I'm pretty sure we need to get Theresa released from those chains. Then we can take her to the police station and let her get cleaned up and fed. As for you Carl I think you better accompany us to the station until we can get the whole thing straightened out."

Carl: "I don't think you should release her. She's working on your pity just like she did to me. She will turn on you at any time. Trust me as God is my witness."

Pete: "Carl. Give me the keys to her manacles. Theresa, you're going to be a good girl aren't you?"

Theresa gave Pete a look of pleading, sweet innocence. "Pete, I would never hurt you. You look so big and strong and I would be forever grateful to have you as my savior."

Carl stepped in front of Pete. Doing his best to block Pete from setting Theresa free. "Pete, if you must set her free take this. If she is truly the spawn of Satan this may protect you." Carl took the small silver cross from around his neck. Pete seemed reluctant at first feeling it was just a crazy act of defiance from Carl but to appease him he let Carl put the cross around his neck.

Pete cautiously approached Theresa. He got down on his knees as he undid Theresa's manacles. She began to purr like a contended kitten as her hands started to lovingly caress Pete's arms with her hands. When the last shackle was released she wrapped her arms around Pete's neck and began to sensually kiss him. She pulled up her tattered outfit to reveal her bare legs as she rubbed one of her legs between Pete's thighs and pushed him onto his back. "Now you shall be my slave and do Satan's bidding. Kill Carl, Ole and the little dog. Then you and I shall rule this village along with my Master Satan!"

Pete was struggling to get free, except he had grown weak under her spell. Big as he was she now had the strength to hold him down.

Carl: "I told you! Ole, we need to bind her hands to get control of her!"

Theresa turned her head to look at us, eyes black as coal and fanged teeth bared in an evil grin. She screamed like a banshee. "Come near me and your friend will die!"

She pulled her top down to reveal her bare breasts, and then she tore open Pete's shirt as she pushed her bare body against him. "I will take him and then he will be my slave!" Suddenly she let out a scream of terror. She sat bolt upright with the shape of the cross from Pete's necklace etched into the skin between her breasts. The shape of the cross spread like the flames of hell across her body. "Carl! You tricked me! Damn you!" her body was soon consumed in flames and then it suddenly turned to ash and fell across Peter's prone body.

Pete jumped to his feet, brushing away Theresa's ashes as best he could. "What the hell!" was all he could say.

Carl: "What the hell is correct. I told you she was possessed."

I looked at Ole and said. "Carl's right. Anyone that would try to attack a cute little dog like me isn't all there."

Ole being the only one that could hear me, just smiled and nodded in agreement.

Carl: "Pete, Ole and even you Tesse. You all saw what just happened. You're my witnesses. Do you still think I broke the law and should be arrested?"

Pete: "Well, there was certainly no damsel in distress. Without a prisoner or even a body I can't really see that I would have anything to charge you with. Other than saving my life with that cross you gave me. As far as I'm concerned the case of the screaming, chain rattling ghosts of St. Catherine's has been investigated and satisfactorily taken care of."

Carl: "What are you going to tell the villagers?"

Ole: "I think boiler and furnace issues is as good an explanation as any. Carl, you get someone in here to replace that old furnace and boiler and I'm sure there will be no more unexplained noises coming from the church. I'll even do my best to get the village to help fund it. I'll explain to them that it is our duty to do so. After all St. Catherine's is a historical landmark and very much a part of Longhall County's and Hedgehoghaven's history."

Carl could hardly thank us enough for taking a major problem off his hands. He shook hands with Ole and Pete and I got a pat on my head as we left St. Catherine's. Carl added in a well-deserved jab as we walked towards our vehicles. "Maybe, next time you will believe the word of a Deacon."

Ole: "Pete, a job well done. Want to go to Chaps or Rocky's for a pint. I'll buy."

Pete: "Thanks for the offer but I think I would like to go home and get out of my ash covered uniform and burn it. Then I'm going to go inside my cottage and cuddle up with my wife and tell her how much I love her."

CHAPTER 18

It was now late November, and Halloween and the case of the possessed faux nun Theresa were things of the past. Luck had been with us twice now. The kids we took to Castle Longhall on Halloween night had kept their mouths shut and no blowback of monsters or endangering children had fell on us. Possessed faux Sister Theresa had vanished into flames and ash and was no longer haunting St. Catherine's. Overall things were looking pretty peaceful and normal in Longhall County and Hedgehoghaven Village. Despite the fact that the County moto was "Where legends live and reality dies."

The sky was overcast, and a typical winter day for this time of year, or so we were told. We decided to spend the evening at Chaps Pub. It was a week night which meant less customers and normally a quiet night for business. We joined Fire Chief Dale, Arcade owner Kelley and Doctor John at their table. The guys were just waiting for a fourth person to show up so they could play doubles at darts. Tonight's game was cricket. Needing a fourth for their game we were drafted as soon as we came through the door.

Our English friends ordered appetizers as they figured Ole was not really English enough to appreciate the fine cuisine they were hungry for. Small talk dominated the conversation when Tessa who was waitressing delivered our appetizers to our table. Maple-Siracha Devil's on horseback, sausage rolls, Angels on horseback and Scotch eggs.

One good thing about Ole and me, we were game to try anything. Once when we were motorcycling through Montana back in the colonies we ate Rocky Mountain Oysters 'bull balls' for those not in the know. We also tried pickled eggs. We both decided deep fried 'bull balls' were far superior then the vinegar soaked pickled eggs. If you really think about it there isn't that much difference from eating something that came from a bulls sack or something that came from a chicken's ass. Really, you should think about that.

A coin was flipped to see who would be partners in the game of cricket. Ole figured he came out well on the flip as he was partnered with Kelley. Kelley not only owned the local arcade but he also ran all the amusement games in the county. He had a reputation as a competent dart player. The stakes for the two out of three game tournament was that the losers had to pay for the appetizers and beer. This was a keen incentive for Kelley to win as his beer consumption was at least 4 to 1 compared to the rest of us. The unusual thing to me was that no matter how much beer Kelley consumed it never seemed to affect him. He was always good natured and he got along with everybody. Overall he was just a nice guy, but so were Dale and John.

I sat on my stool, sneaking a Maple-Siracha Devils on Horseback whenever no one was looking. Basically it is a date stuffed with blue cheese and wrapped with bacon that has a Maple-Siracha glaze. I'm sure some of your health freaks are probably thinking that stuff is really bad for you. However they have dates in them and dates are healthy and good for you. So there. Stuff that in your pipe and smoke it. Whoops, wait, smoking is for sure bad for you. I really don't like this new vegan woke world very much. I'd say sorry if I offended you but I still believe in the American axiom of free speech even if those 'woke' people in the United

States keep flaunting it about their feelings but they don't want to hear about anyone else's. As for England it seems the famous like J.K. Rowling and Jermery Clarkson can't express their opinions without all kinds of 'woke' folk attacking them. Guess what, they have a right to speak their minds and have their own opinions. I say go get 'em I'm behind you all the way.

Watching the cricket game, I could see that Dale and John were no match for the power team of Kelley and Ole. Although, Ole was about the same caliber as Dale and John. Kelley seemed to be holding back some to make the game last a little longer. There was no doubt in my mind that Kelley was master at his trade and could blow all three of the others away anytime he wanted to.

While Ole was waiting for his turn, he sauntered over to the Wurlitzer jukebox and punched the button for 'Only Daddy that'll Walk the Line' by Waylon Jennings. Just good old tail wagging music as far as I was concerned.

Kelley and Ole won the first round of cricket. Dale and John were discussing what strategy to use in the next round as they drank more beer to strengthen their resolve. The door of the pub opened and a cold gust of wind assailed everyone inside.

Pierce, Winton, and Ray rushed inside with rain-soaked slickers and water dripping onto the floor.

Pierce: "There's a nasty norther' brewing out there. The wind has picked up and the rain is coming down in buckets. I was lucky to get the Carolsea into port before it was too late."

Casey: "I don't care what it's like outside! You three get those wet slickers off and hang them up. You're dripping water all over my floor."

Winton: "We need beer! Beer, I say! Make it snappy!"

Casey: "You can ask politely or you can go dry. No more shouting if you want to be served in my pub. If not you three can go back out in the storm and make your way to Rocky's Tavern."

Ray: "Winton didn't mean anything by it Casey. We just docked at the pier after a harrowing experience. Winton, you apologize to Casey and everyone else in here for being so rude."

Winton's face turned red as he blushed with shame. "I'm sorry, folks. I'm just so darn excited about what happened to us."

Pierce: "Winton and Ray are right. We got us a story to tell that you won't bloody believe."

The three of them sat down at the table in the middle of the room. Pierce told everyone to gather round to hear the tale that the three of them were dying to share.

For those of you who are not familiar with these three, I'll give you a brief rundown. Pierce or as he prefers to be called Captain Pierce is the owner and captain of the puffer ship the Carolsea. In this case Pierce is definitely the master spinner of yarns in this little threesome.

Winton and Ray are best friends, and both are avid fishermen and heavy drinkers. Winton owns the restaurant 'In Cod We Trust' which specializes in his own recipe of fish and chips.

He also sells fresh caught fish which he smokes in his own smokers and guards his secret recipe with his life. Winton is sort of short and round and gets excited very easily which shows as his face turns beet red and you would swear he is about to explode with a heart attack at any moment.

Ray is Winton's bosom buddy, and they do almost everything together when it comes to fishing and drinking. Ray owns 'Lovett's Butcher' shop. He is also a heavy drinker. Although the more he drinks the quieter he gets. That may be partially due to the fact that Winton gets rather boisterous as he fills his body with beer. Beer gives Ray a red face that matches Winton's. If the two had lived in the old west of the United States they could have easily fit the description of the red skinned Indians.

Casey brought three pints of beer to the guys, and the story was about to unfold.

Pierce: "What I am about to tell you is the absolute truth. No fibs, no lies, no embellishments. Just plain old fact. Believe it or not this is just the way it happened and Winton and Ray were both there to verify it. Ain't it so mates?"

Winton and Ray both agreed as they guzzled down their beers.

Pierce: "Winton and Ray wanted to come along on a fishing excursion I was making with the Carolsea. The old puffer was in fine meddle. The boiler had been filled with fresh water and we had a good supply of coal to keep her happy.

I had made an inspection the day before we left, and all the nets were in fine condition, and we had plenty of supplies. The weather was good and clear as we left the dock and as we neared the light house I could see two figures standing outside the light house door. As we drew closer I made one out to be the pirate Captain Jack Sparrow. The other was that skinny scraggly dark haired snaggly toothed voodoo lady from Louisiana Marie Laveau.

Now Jack being a friendly sort, gave a tip of his tri-cornered hat and shouted out a hearty farewell and safe journey. Marie on the other hand let out with an 'eeeghh, another man done gone.' Now I realize that sounded a bit like the Bobby Bare song, and it was. Seeing Jack and her together made me wonder just what those two could possibly have in common. Winton and Ray just blew off what she said and asked where I kept the beer. As for me, I took it as a bad omen to the start of our voyage.

Our first day out on the open sea was calm, with a bright sun shining. We had dropped our nets and our cargo hold was quickly filling with fish. As dusk was sneaking up on us we stowed the fishing nets and battened down the hatches for a peaceful night. As the weather cooled a fog began to roll in and settled around the Carolsea. It was a pleasant although a bit damp evening but we still decided to spend some time on deck. Winton got out his guitar and Ray pulled out his squeezebox. I had a few barrels of rum and we were soon drinking and singing 'What do you do with a drunkin' sailor' when one of my crew hollered out. 'Ship off the starboard side Captain and she is on a direct course to ram us!'

Ray stood up and dropped his mug of rum onto the deck as he proclaimed. "I'll be damned! It's a three mast sailing ship Looks like something out of the past. If I wasn't half drunk I'd almost swear it looks like the ship from the stories I've heard about the Flying Dutchman."

Winton joined Ray at the railing. He stared for a moment or so and took a big swig of rum from his tankard. "Piercy, you best come take a look see. I think Ray might be right. The tattered sails and grey worn wood of the hull looks bloody old and scary.'

Of course, I went and joined Winton and Ray at the railing. As the ship loomed large from the fog that now seemed to be moving with it we could see its crew gathered at the rails, while some of them hung like sure footed cats from its riggings. The Captain stood in front of his crew with legs slightly spread and sure footed as he stared us down.

Winton: "Accept me matey's there was something very strange about the crew. Even in the poor light of a foggy evening we could see they had a grey pallor on their skin and some of them seemed to be missing arms and legs and a few even had what looked to be holes blown clean through their bodies."

Ray: "Some of you may think that Winton is exaggerating mates. But I tell you he isn't. Every word of it is true. The crew's clothes were in tatters and I'd swear at the time I could see seaweed hanging from some of them."

Tessa had stopped waitressing, and like everyone else in the pub, she was aptly hanging on every word of the story. I only tell you this for as she heard this last bit she gave out with an astonished gasp.

Pierce: "The guys are right. Even from a distance we could see something strange about that ship and its crew. I ordered for my first mate to take evasive action but no matter what we did that ship was bearing down on us and I thought for sure we were about to meet our maker.

Just as I was sure we were going to be rammed and sunk, the big ship slid alongside of us smooth as could be without so much as a bump of its hull to our hull. It was then that I realized what we were dealing with. You all know what I'm about to tell you don't you?"

Tessa shook her head no, but all the others in the group made a collective murmur that went through the pub like the fog from the story. "The Flying Dutchman."

Pierce: "So it was. The Flying Dutchman. You all know who the captain is?"

Tessa: "No, who is it?" That's what happens when your young I guess.

Once again, the crowd said it in almost hushed tones, as if saying it would bring evil into the pub itself. "Davy Jones."

Pierce: "Aye, none other than himself. Captain Davy Jones. He stood there with the hard shelled skin of a crab. Barnacles attached to parts of his body and what resembled hair hanging from under his hat looked to be mixtures of sea weed and octopus tentacles. His long coat was faded burgundy in color with brass buttons and tattered with age. His knee high boots were dotted with sea urchins. He looked us over as his crew gawked at us like hungry seagulls looking at a catch of fresh fish. Suddenly as if by magic the Captain was aboard the Carolsea. He bellowed out. "What ship do I have the pleasure of boarding and who is the Captain!"

I straightened out my Captain's cap on my head and tugged at my shirt to make myself look more presentable. Captain. You are on board the puffer ship the Carolsea. Home port of Hedgehoghaven, England. I am Captain Pierce. May I inquire your name dear sir? Of course I was pretty sure who he was but I didn't want to presume anything and I surely hoped I was mistaken.

His beady eyes which looked like they belonged to a shark and not a human, stared at me before he spoke.

"I am Captain Davy Jones of the Flying Dutchman. Originally home ported out of Amsterdam, but now our port is the Seven Seas. You may have heard of me and my ship in your travels."

I said. "Indeed I have Captain. It is our pleasure to welcome such a legend as yourself aboard my humble vessel." Of course I didn't mean it but I didn't want to offend him. "May I offer you a drink of rum?"

Davy Jones: "You may. If you have any extra have your men toss a few barrels over to my crew. They have a thirst that is unquenched for any type of refreshment, be it rum or the souls of the living."

Well, you can bet that none of us liked the sound of that. So I told Captain Jones that I would give him all the rum we had on board and even offered our fresh haul of fish but the Carolsea had no living souls on board to spare.

Davy: "If you know your legends your offer may seem generous to you but not to me and my crew. That is not how things work when you meet up with the Flying Dutchman. At least one soul has to come with us before we can depart. If none come willingly we will have to sink your ship and take all of your souls. You have a choice but it is only good until daybreak."

I told Davy that I didn't much like the idea of taking any souls or sinking my ship. I needed to stall for time and try to figure out some way out of this mess. So I offered Davy a few more drinks and suggested we sing some songs and see if there might be some other option available.

Davy: "Take a look at my crew matey. They are hungry for fresh souls to join the crew. Whenever we add a new soul to our crew the crewman with the most seniority can go to his resting place in Davy Jones locker. So you can see that there is no option for you or your crew."

I figured that maybe if I could get Davy drunk enough that I might be able to trick him into going back on board the Flying Dutchman, and we might just be able to escape before he had time to take one of us. Winton, Ray, Davy and me all took a seat on some empty barrels that were on the deck of the Carolsea. I had one of my crew keep the rum flowing. I suggested that Davy might like to join us in another round of singing 'Drunkin' Sailor,' to keep the mood light hearted. Davy had something else in mind.

Davy said drunkin' sailors are always fun to have around if one was on land or even on a ghost ship as the Flying Dutchman that never makes port. "Whenever we take a new soul aboard we always have a great celebration with lots of drink flowing, mostly it's the blood of our new recruit. I think we should have my crew and yours join in a song that is very popular aboard the Dutchman. Let's all join in on singing 'Dead Man's Chest.' Now that's a seafaring song to make a man's blood run warm. Ehh…matey's"

A rousing cheer went up from the crew of the Dutchman. Winton and Ray started playing the tune on their instruments, and soon everyone was singing. I was racking my brain trying to figure out a way to prolong any decision about sacrificing one of my crew. I decided to try a new approach. Davy, I say, have you ever seen the City of Atlantis? Is it real or just a legend?

Davy: "Atlantis. A beautiful place and as real as you and me matey. Some like to think it sank to the bottom of the sea and took all who lived there to their deaths. Couldn't be more untrue matey's. Sure she went down into the sea but it is protected by a large invisible dome and all who live there walk around and enjoy their lives just as they had done before the city disappeared. It is quite an anomaly if I say so myself. Now when I say I been there, I mean I've seen it from outside the dome. Seems they will not let the dead visit their realm. That dome protects them from the undead like me and my crew. I only wish I could get in there. The women are as beautiful as Greek Goddesses. I'd love to have one of them for myself, or a half dozen, one for each day of the week. Then like God above I could be busy for six days and rest up on the seventh day. Haha, what a life for a sailor that would be!"

I offered Davy more rum as I tried to figure some way out of our dilemma. "Enough rum Captain Pierce" he bellowed. The night is waning and it is time for your decision. One of your crew or all of them and the Carolsea goes to my locker at the bottom of the sea.

All of a sudden, the Carolsea started leaning off to the port side of where the Flying Dutchman was lashed to our starboard side. The four of us stood up to see what was causing the list of the Carolsea.

It looked as if Davy and the Dutchman were not the only nightmare we had to contend with. An army of creatures was climbing from the water as they boarded my ship. They were about six-feet tall with bodies similar to a human in shape but they were covered with green scales and their feet and hands were webbed and shaped like large fins. Gills for breathing were located along their cheeks. My first thought was that they resembled the gill men from the old 1954 movie Creature from the Black Lagoon. One of the creatures whose scales were a deeper green than the others seemed to be the leader. They swarmed aboard my ship and soon formed what looked like a line of defense along the railing of the Carolsea as they faced the crew of the Dutchman. The leader of these gill men was soon standing flipper to toe with Davy Jones.

The Gillman looked at Davy as he said. 'Davy Jones, so we meet again."

Davy replied. "That we do, you slimy creature."

Gillman: "I suggest you leave this ship and all on board alone. It will soon be daybreak and you and your crew will melt away like jellyfish rotting on a hot beach."

Davy: "This time you win. We'll depart as per your request. Only because there is not enough time left for us to fulfill the contract with Captain Pierce, just remember this Captain Pierce. We will be waiting for when the time comes to fulfill our bargain."

Gillman: "Make your threats Captain Jones. Just remember this ship the Carolsea. Captain Pierce and his crew are under our protection. Best for you and your crew to forget this one and find new prey. You've got seven oceans to make your search. I would wish you good luck but 'good' is not something I would equate with you and the Flying Dutchman."

Captain Jones had an indignant look on his face as he turned heel and re-boarded the Flying Dutchman. As soon as he had set foot on his ship, he and his crew along with the Flying Dutchman disappeared in a vortex of swirling fog.

I turned to face the Gillman, and I can tell you I was a bit intimated by him.

Winton" "Intimidated? You were scared to death."

Ray: "For sure, you figured we might just have jumped out of the frying pan and into the fire."

Pierce: "Ok, I'll admit I was a bit worried. We had just been rescued from Davy Jones and now we had these unusual creatures swarming about our ship. I finally mumbled out a 'thank you' and then asked 'what do you want from us?"

All I could think of at the moment was 'shiver me timbers' we have gone from one threat to another. These creatures looked as if they would love to have us for lunch. I don't mean as guests, I mean as the main course.

Gillman: "There is no need to be afraid. We mean you no harm. We came to rescue you and your ship from Davy Jones and his undead crew. We have met up with the Captain before and he knows that Neptune the ruler of the Seven Seas will take our side before his so he has no choice but to back down if we should meet in a standoff. Our kind have colonies in all the seven seas and we of course give our allegiance to Neptune. The Flying Dutchman and Captain Davy Jones are only one ship, one captain and a crew of the undead. They owe their allegiance only to Hades as they do their best to collect souls to feed the fires of hell."

Pierce: "We all thank you. May I ask why you decided to help us?"

Gillman: "You come for the port of Hedgehoghaven in Longhall County. Some of our kind have taken refuge in the ruins of Longhall Castle. An underground river runs beneath the Castle and the nearby Easton Mine which allows our kind easy access to the sea. Aaron Long of Longhall County allowed us and others who do not fit into the society of humans a safe haven in the old castle. For this all of our kind are grateful although the majority of us prefer the oceans and lagoons for our homes. We shall leave you in peace. I hope you have a safe voyage home. As for the Flying Dutchman I do not believe it will ever bother you again for Davy Jones now knows you are under the protection of Neptune."

I asked if there was anything we could do to repay the gill men. Their leader asked if they could have some wine and a song before they departed. I didn't have any wine on board, however I told them I did have some rum.

Gillman: "That will do. Now have your musicians play 'Tiny Bubbles in the Wine' for us. Then we shall be on our way."

Pierce, Winton, and Ray sat in silence as the rest of us did our best to digest what we had just been told. It was so quiet in the pub you could have heard a dog fart, and maybe I did, I just don't remember, but the crowd dissipated pretty quickly.

Constable Queen Bee was present and had heard the whole thing. "Balderdash. If any of you village idiots believe that you should be locked up in a loony bin and I'd be glad to put you there and throw away the key."

Tessa: "I liked the story and I believe them."

Winton and Ray in unison. "It's true, every word of it. We were there and we witnessed the whole thing."

Queen: "You two already said you were drinking rum before and during your supposed brush with the Flying Dutchman. Now your drunk again on beer and Pierce sure ain't no stranger to drinking. Tall tales and vivid imagination fueled by alcohol is the only tale you three have to tell. I should lock all three of you up until you're sober and then I'll beat the truth out of you."

If nothing else, the story made for some lively discussion for the rest of the night. I wasn't feeling to well and asked Ole if we could leave early and go back to the cottage.

That night Ole and I slipped into bed, and I curled up close to Ole as he wrapped an arm around me. It was a safe comfortable feeling. I was happy and content. "Ole, I'm feeling really old and tired."

Ole: "You've got a right to be tired, after all your fifteen years old. Just remember this. You're the best partner ever. I've never seen you get mad or angry. You're always happy to be with me and I'm happy to be with you. I love you with all my heart and every night you are in my prayers."

I feel the same about you. I love you. I curled in close and shut my eyes. Then my heart slowed. I saw a bright light and my dog brother and sister Sven and Lena beckoned me to join them in heaven. I watched with Sven and Lena on our heavenly perch as Ole stood over my grave at the side of the cottage. Tears streamed down his face and it broke my heart. But God reassured me that someday we would be back together.

www.ingramcontent.com/pod-product-compliance
Lightning Source LLC
Chambersburg PA
CBHW071509150726
48000CB00002B/506